Working Intersubjectively

Contextualism in Psychoanalytic Practice

Psychoanalytic Inquiry Book Series

Working Intersubjectively

Contextualism in Psychoanalytic Practice

DONNA M. ORANGE

GEORGE E. ATWOOD

ROBERT D. STOLOROW

THE ANALYTIC PRESS

1997   Hillsdale, NJ   London

First paperback printing 2001

Published by
The Analytic Press, Inc.
Editorial Offices:
101 West Street
Hillsdale, NJ 07642

Index by Leonard S. Rosenbaum

Library of Congress Cataloging-in-Publication Data

Orange, Donna M.
Working intersubjectively : contextualism in psychoanalytic practice / Donna M. Orange, George E. Atwood, Robert D. Stolorow.
        p   cm. -- (Psychoanalytic inquiry book series ; v. 17) Includes bibliographical references and index· ISBN 0-88163-360-7
        1. Psychoanalysis. 2. Intersubjectivity. 3. Context effects (Psychology) I. Atwood, George E. I1. Stolorow, Robert D. III. Title. IV. Series·
        [DNLM: 1. Psychoanalytic Theory. 2. Psychoanalytic Therapy--methods. W1 PS427F v. 17 1997 / WM 460 063w 1997] RC506.07   1997/2001
        616.89'17'01~c21
        DNLM/DLC
        tor Library of Congress   97-25312
                                                                        CIP

Printed in the United States of America

10 9 8 7 6 5 4 3 2 1

To all who think and work contextually

Contents

Preface

The development of the intersubjective perspective in psychoanalysis so far has had four movements, each punctuated by a book. In the first, *Faces in a Cloud* (Stolorow and Atwood, 1979), having demonstrated through psychobiographical studies that psychoanalytic metapsychologies derive profoundly from the personal, subjective worlds of their creators, we concluded that what psychoanalysis needs is a theory of subjectivity itself, a unifying framework that can account not only for the phenomena that other theories address but also for the theories themselves. In the second, *Structures of Subjectivity* (Atwood and Stolorow, 1984), we introduced the concept of an intersubjective field—the system formed by differently organized, reciprocally interacting subjective worlds—as the fundamental theoretical construct for this framework. In the third, *Psychoanalytic Treatment* (Stolorow, Brandchaft, and Atwood, 1987), we applied the intersubjectivity principle to an array of important clinical issues, such as analysis of transference and resistance, therapeutic action, and treatment of borderline and psychotic states. In the fourth, *Contexts of Being* (Stolorow and Atwood, 1992), we circled back to four foundational pillars of psychoanalytic theory—the unconscious, mind-body relations, trauma, and fantasy—and resituated them from an intersubjective perspective. Picking up on the title of this last book, we now offer a fifth movement, a book devoted to a broad-based philosophy of psychoanalytic practice that we refer to as *contextualism*.

The first chapter presents an overview of the basic principles of intersubjectivity theory and illustrates their clinical application through a vignette. In the second we offer a contextualist critique of the concept of psychoanalytic technique, and in the third we do the same for the myth of analytic neutrality. The fourth chapter examines the intersubjective contexts of extreme states of psychological disintegration. In the fifth and final chapter we explore what it means, philosophically and clinically, to think and work contextually. Our hope, embedded in each of these chapters, is to convey to our readers the essential ingredients of a contextualist sensibility.

Working Intersubjectively

Contextualism in Psychoanalytic Practice

– 1 –

Intersubjectivity Theory and the Clinical Exchange

> The person with understanding does not know and judge as one who stands apart and unaffected; but rather, as one united by a specific bond with the other, he thinks with the other and undergoes the situation with him.
>
> —Hans-Georg Gadamer
> *Truth and Method*

By intersubjectivity theory we mean the psychoanalytic theory articulated in *Structures of Subjectivity* (Atwood and Stolorow, 1984) and developed in *Psychoanalytic Treatment* (Stolorow, Brandchaft, and Atwood, 1987), in *Contexts of Being* (Stolorow and Atwood, 1992), and in *Emotional Understanding* (Orange, 1995). An early formulation of this viewpoint said that "psychoanalysis seeks to illuminate phenomena that emerge within a specific psychological field constituted by the intersection of two subjectivities—that of the patient and that of the analyst" (Atwood and Stolorow, 1984, p. 64).

Intersubjectivity theory is a metatheory of psychoanalysis. It examines the field—two subjectivities in the system they create and from which they emerge—in any form of psychoanalytic treatment. Because of this focus, intersubjectivity theory also implies a contextualist view of development and of pathogenesis:

3

Psychological development and pathogenesis are best conceptualized in terms of the specific intersubjective contexts
that shape the developmental process and that facilitate or
obstruct the child's negotiation of critical developmental
tasks and successful passage through developmental
phases. The observational focus is the evolving psychological field constituted by the interplay between the differently
organized subjectivities of child and caretakers [p. 65].

Intersubjectivity theory intends to describe the emergence and
modification of subjectivity, and defines these processes as irreducibly relational.

It is important to distinguish this use of the terms "intersubjective" and "intersubjectivity" from several related ideas. First,
intersubjectivity theorists intend a relatedness that can exist
between any two people as subjects. Thus, these terms do not
refer primarily to a developmental achievement. Stern (1985),
for example, describes a stage and process of recognition of
another's subjectivity as connected and responsive to one's
own. This mutual recognition may be a late achievement in the
intersubjective field of an analysis, especially in patients like
those described by Guntrip (1969) and Kohut (1971), and thus
differs from our contextualist conception of an intersubjective
field.

In addition, intersubjectivity theory differs from systems
theory, as defined, for example, in the family-systems theory of
Bowen and his collaborators[1] (Kerr and Bowen, 1988).
Intersubjectivity requires subjectivity, or rather two or more subjectivities, and retains its focus on the interplay between differently organized subjectivities. We cannot work within the
intersubjective field and simultaneously step outside the field to
describe it, as family-systems theorists attempt to do, from a
God's-eye view.

This impossibility may also account for what appears as psychoanalytic disinterest in empirical research. Positivist philosophers like Grunbaum (1984) and psychoanalysts like Spence
(1993) find psychoanalysis unscientific, but they have misunder-

---

1. We show in a later chapter, nevertheless, that more process-oriented
forms of systems theory are compatible with our point of view.

stood the essential nature of the intersubjective field. Even the best case studies can only feebly attempt to capture the feel of a particular intersubjective field, or of an analytic couple. We must examine the theories, prejudices, and assumptions that form our own subjectivity, but we can work psychoanalytically and understand psychoanalytically only from within the intersubjective field.

Third, for similar reasons, intersubjectivity theory differs from interpersonalism. Intersubjectivity theory concerns itself little with interpersonalist concerns like who is doing what to whom, with gambits and control. What interpersonalists call "participant observation" requires, we believe, maintaining an external perspective that interferes with "undergoing the situation" with the patient (Gadamer, 1975b). In our view, relational contexts are mutually constitutive: as students of aesthetics sometimes say, the writer creates the reader and the reader brings the writer into being. Intersubjectivity theory, although interested in the *experience* of interaction and agency, resembles more closely those currents in relational thinking that emphasize development (Bollas, 1987; Ghent, 1992; Winnicott, 1958) and conversation between differently organized and inevitably subjective perspectives (Aron, 1996; Orange, 1995).

On the other hand, intersubjectivity theory transcends the Freudian view of human beings. In classical theory we are self-contained bundles of better or more poorly harnessed sexual and aggressive instincts, some directed at "objects." Intersubjectivity theory sees humans as organizers of experience, as subjects. *It views psychoanalysis as the dialogic attempt of two people together to understand one person's organization of emotional experience by making sense together of their intersubjectively configured experience* (Orange, 1995).

BASIC THEORETICAL CONCEPTS
AND THEIR HISTORY

Although intersubjectivity theory is a recent arrival on the psychoanalytic scene, its roots appear in early phenomenology. Like Freud, Husserl studied with the philosopher Brentano, who unrelentingly emphasized the experience of the intentional subject. Unlike Freud, who—at least intermittently—embraced scientific empiricism, Husserl and later philosophers of subjectivity claimed that all experience is subjective experience.

The original authors of psychoanalytic intersubjectivity theory, influenced as well by personology theory (Murray, 1938) and by their own researches into the subjective origins of personality theories (Atwood and Stolorow, 1993), recognized in Kohut's work the more radical perspective needed. Though he welcomed and promoted exchange between psychoanalysis and the other humanistic disciplines, Kohut (1959) insisted that the entire domain of psychoanalytic inquiry is subjective experience. He implicitly rejected drive theory, along with metapsychological constructs generally. The only data for psychoanalytic understanding, Kohut believed, are those that are accessible by introspection and empathy. Intersubjectivity theory does criticize particular aspects of self-psychological theory, such as the concepts of transmuting internalization via optimal frustration and a preexisting nuclear self. Nevertheless, it completely accepts self psychology's most fundamental tenet, its definition of the sources of psychoanalytic inquiry and understanding as well as its conviction that self-experience is radically context-dependent—that is, rooted in specific contexts of relatedness.

In the early 1980s Bernard Brandchaft, who brought extensive and intensive understanding of British relational theories, began to make important contributions to the evolution of intersubjectivity theory. The phenomenological approach that emerged from the studies collected in *Faces in a Cloud* (Stolorow and Atwood, 1979), with its thoroughgoing emphasis on the development and maintenance of the organization of experience, thus moved toward a fully intersubjective conception. In this view, all selfhood—including enduring patterns of personality and pathology—develops and is maintained within, and as a function of, the interplay between subjectivities. Conversely the field itself consists of the relatedness between subjectivities. The people may be parent and child, siblings, analyst and patient, spouses, or other combinations. Intersubjectivity theory sees pathologies, from phobias through psychoses, in these terms. In other words, it radically refuses to place the origins or the continuance of psychopathology solely within the patient. This point of view, therefore, differs with drive theory in all its variants. Because self psychology and phenomenology have taught us to emphasize subjective experience, we also differ with interpersonalists who locate difficulties in living in the patient's desire for control, in repetitive enactments of earlier relational patterns, or in disavowal of responsibility. Instead, we study the intersubjective conditions, or emotional context, in which particular subjective configurations arise and are maintained.

The principal components of subjectivity, in our view, are the organizing principles, whether automatic and rigid, or reflective and flexible. These principles, often unconscious, are the emotional conclusions a person has drawn from lifelong experience of the emotional environment, especially the complex mutual connections with early caregivers. Until these principles become available for conscious reflection, and until new emotional experience leads a person to envision and expect new forms of emotional connection, these old inferences will thematize the sense of self. This sense of self includes convictions about the relational consequences of possible forms of being. A person may feel, for example, that any form of self-articulation or differentiation will invite ridicule or sarcasm.

Within this perspective, we have attempted to rethink such fundamental psychoanalytic ideas as the unconscious. The "prereflective unconscious" is the home of those organizing principles, or emotional convictions, that operate automatically and out of awareness. They arise as emotional inferences a child draws from intersubjective experience in the family of origin. These principles may concern relatedness, as in "I must adapt to others' needs (moods, expectations, and so on) if I am to retain significant emotional ties." They may also consist in a fundamental sense of self, still intersubjectively configured: "I will never amount to anything," "I am always a burden," "I am worthless and good-for-nothing." Such organizing principles are sometimes direct quotations from parents who nickname their children "Mad Mary" or "Terrible Theresa" or "good-for-nothing." More often, these principles are emotional inferences drawn as the child attempts to organize some sense of self out of chaotic, traumatic, or more subtly confusing early and later relational experience.

We (Stolorow and Atwood, 1992) have also described a dynamic unconscious. This consists of emotional information, once consciously known, that had to be "sequestered," or forgotten, because it created conflict for the subject. In particular, the memory would threaten the tie to caregivers on whom the child needed to depend. This form of unconsciousness is dynamic, as in Freudian theory, because the effects of such early experience, unavailable for reflection, continue to appear as repetitive troubles in an adult's life. Memories of parental cruelty that conflict with needed idealizations are obvious examples.

Finally, the "unvalidated unconscious" describes those aspects of subjective life that could never fully become experience because they never found a validating response in the emotional environment. Often aspects of one's talents and interests, one's character, as well as of the crises and quandries of one's emotional life have never found the recognition they needed to become fully real for the person.

THE CLINICAL EXCHANGE

An intersubjective understanding of psychopathology and of unconsciousness has important consequences for psychoanalytic practice. Psychoanalysis will consist in the mutual creation of an emotional environment, an intersubjective field, in which it is safe to explore together those "regions" of unconsciousness that make up the problematic aspects of subjectivity. The interplay of transference and countertransference (or cotransference, Orange, 1994), the organizing activity of both patient and analyst within the analytic experience, makes up the intersubjective field of the analysis. The joint effort to understand both past and present organizing activity as a function of the experience of particular intersubjective fields means that past and present are always dialogically involved, implicitly at least; with those who cannot even try to understand the past and have no access at all to it, explicit dialogue between past and present may be many years ahead.

The intersubjective field of the analysis, made possible by the emotional availability of both analyst and patient, becomes a developmental second chance for the patient (Orange, 1995). New, more flexible organizing principles can emerge, now accessible to reflection, so that the patient's experiential repertoire becomes enlarged, enriched, and more complex. Under severe stress, old organizations of experience may return, but now a person can recognize them and relativize them by reference to their origins in past relational experience.

In the remainder of this chapter we illustrate the clinical exchange from the standpoint of intersubjectivity theory. In our view, there is no distinct body of clinical theory or of "technical" recommendations to be derived from intersubjectivity theory. Rather, the intersubjective perspective introduces a more general characterization of all psychoanalytic work from within any specific clinical theory. Because each treatment includes an analyst with a point of view, different kinds of intersubjective fields develop in classical, interpersonal, or self-psychological treatments (Orange, 1995), as well as in each psychoanalytic pair. From a clinical point of view, intersubjectivity is not so much a theory as it is a sensibility. It is an attitude of continuing sensitivity to the inescapable interplay of observer and observed. It assumes that instead of entering and immersing ourselves in the experience of another, we join the other in the intersubjective space. Each participant in the psychoanalytic field brings an organized and organizing emotional history to the process. This means that although the analysis is always for the patient, the emotional history and psychological organization of patient and analyst are equally important to the understanding of any clinical exchange. (This idea is explained further in a chapter on cotransference in *Emotional Understanding*, Orange, 1995.) What we inquire about or interpret or leave alone depends upon who we are. The analytic process, as relational theorist Lewis Aron (1996) has explained, is mutually constituted but asymmetrical. One participant is primarily there as helper, healer, and inquirer. The other chiefly seeks relief from emotional suffering. (The Latin root of *patient* means to suffer, undergo, or bear. The word may also be related to the Greek *pathos*.) In the developmental process we call psychoanalysis, one is primarily guide and the other seeks to organize and reorganize experience in less painful and more creative ways. Nevertheless, each is a full participant and contributor to the process that emerges.

The following case material illustrates the ways in which the analyst's organization of experience interacts with that of the patient to form a unique and indissoluble psychological system. This analyst's theories, a particular amalgam of self psychology, attachment theory, and intersubjectivity theory, are always present and formative. Even more, personal history shapes and limits any analyst's capacities for empathic-introspective understanding, and in particular, both expands and constricts the extent of emotional availability to any given patient. This means we must be much more self-revealing in describing clinical work than is typical in psychoanalytic writing. The case is presented not to show an example of optimal "technique." Rather we intend to demonstrate how conjunctions and disjunctions between the subjective worlds of patient and analyst sometimes facilitate and sometimes impede the process of treatment.

BACKGROUND

Kathy, a 33-year-old assistant professor of literature and women's studies, came to treatment after her most recent period of severe depression, for which she had begun to take antidepressants, which seemed to help, except that she often forgot to take them. Of Italian-American descent, she was much the youngest of three children of their mother, who had died of breast cancer when Kathy was 6, and a father who remarried when Kathy was 13. She lived with her boyfriend of several years, who wished she could have more fun and be less serious.

This is all we knew together when Kathy began treatment. No one in her family had been willing to speak about the past, and Kathy had not wanted to know more. But now she felt ready to ask why she fell into bouts of deep depression. She called and wrote to the hospital where her mother had twice stayed in psychiatric units, and, despite much bureaucratic bumbling, persuaded the records office to send her mother's discharge summary to her analyst. It finally arrived about three months into the treatment. By this time, her analyst had understood that Kathy's mother was the central figure that sustained her in her imagination. Reading the story of her mother's two attempts to kill Kathy filled the analyst with dread. What would happen now? What would be the impact of knowing that the central person in her life had tried to murder her? Would she want to kill herself? When Kathy arrived for her session, they decided to read the report together. Before they started, her analyst made sure the patient would not be alone after the session. The sense of

Kathy as the younger sister whom her analyst must protect probably began at this time.

Kathy's mother had been diagnosed with cancer when Kathy was still an infant, became seriously depressed, began to act "crazy," and after a suicide attempt, was hospitalized when Kathy was five. According to the hospital records—which did not make it clear who provided the information—the mother had intended to commit suicide twice, when Kathy was three and again at five, and tried to take her daughter along, that is, tried to kill her, so Kathy would not have to grow up motherless (as the mother had). On both occasions, Kathy had refused to take the pills (patient and analyst connect this with her difficulty remembering to take antidepressants). Perhaps, somehow knowing the mother would not commit suicide if she had to leave her daughter behind, Kathy was trying to save her mother by refusing to take the pills. Kathy had no direct memory of these incidents, but had terrifying nightmares and recurrent immobilizing depressions.

Later, Kathy's brothers told her that the mother often beat the middle child severely with a belt that always hung in the kitchen. Kathy remembers the belt hanging there—and that this brother tormented Kathy, who seemed to escape the mother's wrath. After the mother's death, the oldest brother cared for Kathy, but when Kathy was 13, this brother married and moved out, and their father remarried. An older male cousin who lived nearby molested Kathy almost daily for several years, when she was 6 through 12. Believing she was doing something terribly wrong, she felt she could tell no one. Kathy later moved, however, and in that process found and brought to treatment a diary written when she was 14. Here she had repeatedly written out her longing for "mommy," her awareness of the effects of the incest on her ability to trust boys, and her desire to be dead. She had not remembered any of this, or even that the diary existed. After this session, Kathy remembered bringing the diary, but had no memory of the contents, and seemed surprised when reminded.

The early years of treatment involved her analyst's frequently reminding Kathy of her own history—both recent and remote—which she seemed alternately to know and not know. She came in with a problem: "I can only have sex if I go away in my mind." Patient and analyst worked together on finding meanings—in this instance she had completely forgotten the incest and a rape in her college years—and she went away feeling enlightened. Sometimes, as in this case, the symptom disappeared. Then she came in saying she was doing well and was wondering why she was in treatment. "Oh, but I had a bad Saturday—so depressed I couldn't get out of bed all day." Then the wondering and reminding process began again. If the analyst said anything to indicate that Kathy had a very rough start in life, she seemed surprised. "Oh, do you really think so?"

The analyst's history was both similar and different. The oldest, and thus the caregiver, of a troubled family of ten children, she had survived by hard work, reading, and dissociation. Like Kathy, she had difficulty remembering early troubles and connecting them to feelings in the present. A particular point of intersection was the analyst's having left home when her youngest sisters were three and five, and a strong sense of having abandoned them to a terrible situation. Kathy—who nearly died at those same ages—felt much like one of these younger sisters and evoked the analyst's caregiving and protectiveness. Though Kathy knew nothing of this history, she felt immediately that her analyst was a kindred spirit, in her words, "a wild woman." They developed their own humor together—the private jokes that are often part of specific intersubjective fields. Kohut might have called this a "twinship transference," and surely it was; the point is that the analyst's particular self-experience was an enormous contributor to the particular intersubjective field of this treatment, that is, to the way patient and analyst played and worked together. The clinical material is not dramatic, but the analyst's inquiries and responses—inquiry is a form of response that expresses the shape and limits of an analyst's emotional availability and understanding—were shaped by a particular subjectivity. They were not simple applications of any so-called rules of technique.

The disjointed quality of the conversation is common in work with very dissociative patients. This quality makes it harder for a reader to follow, but it also brings the reader into the emotional context of the experience with Kathy.

The main point about this treatment, from an intersubjective point of view, is that the analyst's awareness of, and struggles with, dissociation made possible the awareness of, and relentless work with, Kathy's. We might compare this empathic process to an analog search, in the sense that Kathy's demons (another patient calls them the "trolls"), or automatic ways of organizing emotional experience, were already familiar to the analyst. A secondary point is that the analyst, historically situated herself, had to be emotionally available to go through Kathy's traumatic history with her. Then it became possible to help Kathy to integrate this history and its effects, and to develop a relatively continuous, cohesive, and valued sense of herself.

SESSION EARLY IN THE SECOND YEAR

Kathy: [Puzzled tone] I have been swinging in and out of depression—trapped—not as severe. Brian [her partner] has been really good. Strange not being there. Housework—Tim [brother eight years older] used to make chores so terrible. . . .

Analyst: [Searching for clues to the depression and the disjointed speech] Housework—can you tell me more about that?

Kathy: [Still puzzled] I don't know why I can't feel anything.

Analyst: [Trying to find context] Just like the last two sessions—the first parts when you couldn't think why you were coming here.

Kathy: [More lively tone] I had an interesting conversation with my friend Jim last week. He thinks abused children blame themselves because normal children are naturally cuddly, needing touch, and he read that the touch receptors in the brain are especially sensitive when children are young. He thinks these natural needs are why we blame ourselves for however people touched us. What do you think of that?

Analyst: Well, we do know babies and children need to be touched and held. Do you mean if kids are hit or molested, they feel shame or blame themselves, like "you asked for it" because of their natural needs?

Kathy: Yes, maybe that's why you can't talk yourself out of it, or say it wasn't your fault, even when you know that.

Analyst: What mostly gives you that feeling?

Kathy: My cousin, I guess. . . . I wish I could remember my mother more, what she looked like, her facial expressions. I really don't remember much—I know she had

red hair, tons of freckles, and her body shape, everyone says, was kind of like mine. [The analyst guessed
that this switch from the cousin to the mother con-
nects with the sense expressed in her childhood diary.
If her mother had lived, she might have been protected from the incest, so that when she remembered
the molestation, she immediately tried to retrieve a
connection to her mother.]

Analyst: But you don't have much sense of her personality, or
how she was with you? [Trying to help her articulate
the loss]

Kathy: No, I wish I could remember.

Analyst: How would that help?

Kathy: Then I could feel sad for the child that I was and not
have to hear that voice: STOP FEELING SORRY FOR YOUR-
SELF.

Analyst: Whose voice is that?

Kathy: That's just what I was wondering. How can I remember? I have such a hard time remembering. [Seemed
lost]

Analyst: [Shifting into didactic mode, trying to help her
become oriented—both analyst and patient were
teachers.] Well, there are lots of ways—dreams, your
writing and poetry, fleeting thoughts, and sometimes
the stuff that goes on between you and me.

Kathy: What do you mean?

Analyst: Sometimes I will seem like someone who has been
important to you, maybe someone who has hurt you,
and that can be a way of remembering. I might say or
do something that will trigger forms of memory.

Kathy: You don't hurt me. But I do sometimes feel: I don't
need this. Why am I coming here? What is she talking
about, that bad things happened to me? I'm just fine.
Then later in the session we get into things. [A colleague pointed out to the analyst that Kathy was terri-
fied of becoming attached to her, longing to do so, and
deeply ashamed of this longing.]

Analyst: Why do you think that happens?

Kathy: I don't know.

Analyst: [Trying to prime the pump, as discussed in the emotional availability chapter of Orange, 1995, where the

parent or therapist sends up trial balloons so that the child or patient can try them out. The analyst's contribution to this intersubjective predicament probably came from the expectation, a product of the analyst's own developmental context, that no one could possibly want to be attached to her. Slow to perceive attachment longings, she unconsciously avoided the attachment issue and missed some of the triggers in the transference for the dissociative phenomena.] Maybe being here with me—your "memory bank"—reminds you of when things were so overwhelming for you that you had to go away from yourself to keep from losing your mind. Or, more recently, when you had to go away during sex. What do you think?

Kathy: I think we are getting somewhere. Maybe I'm afraid of what I will feel if I don't numb out or go away before I come here. I want to remember, but I'm scared to remember. . . .

TWO YEARS LATER
(AFTER A THREE-WEEK BREAK)

Kathy: How are you? How was your vacation?
Analyst: Good, very good. How have you been?
Kathy: OK, I guess. I don't know what's been going on. I can't feel anything. I don't know why I'm here. [Same discomfort as before] I think about cutting back on sessions because I'm OK. I'm really much better. I have decided I have to take the Zoloft. When I forget, I go way down again and can hardly get out of bed or stop crying. But I don't know what to talk about here.
Analyst: So the underlying trouble is still there? [She nods.] But we've lost contact enough these past weeks that you can't imagine or feel any way to work on it here with me? [The analyst again not picking up on how dangerous Kathy's attachment longings are to her and how they trigger the dissociative states]
Kathy: I don't even know what it is. I just get horribly depressed.

Analyst: So if you can just feel better, and keep out of being in bed all the time, things are OK?

Kathy: No, now that you say it that way. I'm still really worried about what happened at work. That was so terrible, and it's pretty recent too. [She had told this story just before vacation.]

Analyst: You mean your colleague who came on to you and you didn't know what to do or how to tell him no.

Kathy: [Very somber] Yes, I can't believe I didn't know what to do. I feel so embarrassed and ashamed. I just let things happen. I don't understand it myself, and even if I did, I couldn't explain it because that would be like making excuses, and there is no excuse for something like that. And I've let things happen like that many times before.

Analyst: So you're worried about how to manage with this colleague, but even more about what goes on with you that you let these things happen.

Kathy: Yes, I feel completely pulled in. I know somewhere in me that it's all wrong, but I can't use that knowledge at all when something like this is going on. [Sounding puzzled] I just mindlessly give in and feel awful afterwards.

Analyst: It reminds me of your dreams where your legs give out from under you. [Recurrent theme in her dreams, often when she was trying to get away from a dangerous situation, or when she was trying to challenge someone. They had often discussed this aspect of her dreams.]

Kathy: Yes, it is like that.

Analyst: As if you can't use the part of yourself that would walk out of a situation that's bad for you or that you've felt drawn into.

Kathy: So why is that? I just don't understand it.

Analyst: Well, let's think about other times in your life when you may have felt helpless to prevent what was going on, even when you felt something was terribly wrong. When you were small, you saw your mother running naked in the street, and another time saw her threatening your father with an ax.

Kathy: [Looking horrified] I had forgotten those things. But I don't connect them with this.

Analyst: OK. Well, what about how you felt when you were being molested by Anthony almost every day for seven years, and felt it was wrong, but didn't know how to make it stop, and had no one to turn to?

Kathy: [Nodding thoughtfully] Yes, it's like that. That's how it feels. I guess I need to work more on that, to tell you more about that, but it's so hard. I don't want to think about it.

Analyst: So much shame?

Kathy: Oh, yes. Well, I guess I'll have to keep coming here. I have to do this work. I can't keep on being like this. I just keep getting into trouble and letting people hurt me.

Analyst: So you will be here next week?

Kathy: Oh, yes.

She missed the next two sessions, but called to say she had not remembered until she was nearly home and it was too late. When she did come in, she painfully recounted some of what she remembered about the incest. She then remembered that the cousin had sometimes brought his friends to participate, and that she was sometimes pinned down. She believed that she would never again allow anyone to mistreat her sexually, and was quite exultant about this.

COMMENTARY

From an intersubjective point of view, all clinical work involves and takes place in the field formed by the interplaying of two subjective worlds. In this case, patient and analyst are similar, different, and complementary. Their related experience of dissociation both facilitated and impeded the analytic process. On one hand, the analyst's sensitivity to dissociative phenomena provided a comfortable and useful focus and interpretive lens or perspective. On the other hand, the analyst did not consider or recognize how dissociative processes were triggered in the transference by dangerous and shame-inducing attachment longings, because the analyst could not envision herself as being so centrally important to the patient—a legacy of the analyst's history of developmental trauma.

Though similar in dissociative tendencies, and in many tastes and interests, Kathy and her analyst differ in family position and in many of the ways they organize experience. The intersection allowed them to create a space where the unbelievable could be explored together, could be known in various ways, and could begin to be integrated. The analyst might be the big brother who did not abuse her and to whom she could turn in times of trouble, or the big brother she needed to avoid and who "makes her do work." Gradually they will be able to recognize and to reorganize Kathy's profound sense that attachment to an older woman is very dangerous. What they do together is a product of their experience in the unique intersubjective field they create together.

It might be argued that nothing in this treatment is unique to the intersubjective perspective. This is surely true. Intersubjectivity theory is not a set of prescriptions for clinical work. It is a sensibility that continually takes into account the inescapable interplay of the two subjects in any psychoanalysis. It radically rejects the notion that psychoanalysis is something one isolated mind does to another, or that development is something one person does or does not do. Working intersubjectively is exploring together for the sake of healing. Each particular analyst creates with each particular patient the opportunity—often, as in this instance, the first opportunity—to integrate and make sense of a painful and confusing life.

– 2 –

Beyond Technique
Psychoanalysis as a
Form of Practice

> Genuine creation is precisely
> that for which we can give no
> prescribed technique or recipe.
> —Barrett
> *The Illusion of Technique*

Many observers of psychoanalysis, as well as some of its participants, have thought that Freud was mistaken in taking his creative attempt to understand emotional suffering to be a science in the tradition of the exact sciences (Bouveresse, 1995). Fewer have noticed that Freud and his followers have also misunderstood psychoanalytic practice as technique. The two misconceptions are related, because both assume that all relevant variables can be controlled; ever since the articulation of the uncertainty principle in physics, we realize that this condition does not exist completely, even in the realm of material things. Practice, on the contrary, is characteristic of work with human beings with minds. The realm of the mental is thoroughly incomplete, indefinite, and open. It is the field of practice, or as Aristotle would have said, of practical wisdom. Although the classical principles of multiple function and of overdetermination respect this difference between matter and mind, as does contemporary relational psychoanalysis with its "postmodern" attitudes, the view of clinical work as technique has remained pervasive and seriously harmful. Our remaining chapters illustrate the alternative mode of thinking about clinical work that we propose.

Technē is the Greek word for the kind of knowledge needed to make something (Aristotle). It describes both the explicit rules and the tacit knowledge (Polanyi, 1958) involved in a craft like carpentry or plumbing or surgery. Distinct from the art or science to which it is related, technique is often a necessary but not a sufficient condition for their full realization.[1] When we say that an artist has great technical skill, we are often damning by faint praise. We are contrasting superb technique with artistry.

Technique, as Barrett (1979) points out, resembles the kind of automatic decision procedure we expect from a well-functioning machine. In his words,

> All that we desire from a machine of this kind is that it go through the routines written into it. The last thing we want from it is that it be creative or inventive in any way. When your automobile starts to sound in the morning as if its starting up were a matter of improvisation or invention, it is usually time to trade it in [p. 23].

An ideal of modern science that has great influence in our field involves just such reduction of thought to a methodical testing of hypotheses. The creative process involved in generating the hypotheses themselves thus becomes an invisible adjunct to method and technique.

Freud, desiring that psychoanalysis command the respect accorded to the exact sciences in his time, declared that it was one.[2] He saw that scientific knowledge often carries associated

---

1. Gadamer (1975b) notes that where early hermeneutics viewed itself as a set of rules for interpreting texts, modern hermeneutics concerns the practice of understanding. In modern science, he believes, "the concept of technology displaced that of practice" (p. 556).

2. Freud, like so many modern thinkers after Descartes, believed in the unity of science. Descartes compared all knowledge (or science) to a house that needed a secure foundation, and to a tree that needed healthy roots. If the underpinnings were solid and certain, so was the rest of knowledge, including the realms of the productive and the practical. This meant that the same kind of truth and the same degree of certainty should be sought in all disciplines. Aristotle, on the contrary, like many contemporary thinkers, believed that each kind of inquiry has its appropriate degree of certainty, and in particular, that the exactness-requiring methods appropriate to the study of such disciplines as mathematics were unsuited for politics, ethics, or esthetics.

technical applications, and from the beginning he thought psychoanalytic work consists of techniques. He frequently referred to dream interpretation as a technique (Freud, 1900). Later, eager to protect the reputation of his young "science" from scandal, he elaborated recommendations for psychoanalytic technique. These concerned anonymity, abstinence, neutrality, and the use of the couch. Further elaborated by Freudians and Kleinians (Bergmann and Hartman, 1976; Etchegoyen, 1991), the recommendations became rules and persist as our collective "psychoanalytic superego" to this day. Despite the creative ferment and dissent in psychoanalysis from Ferenczi to the present, these rules have formed a psychoanalytic backbone and have often formed the "common ground," to use Wallerstein's term, among widely diverging schools of psychoanalytic thinking. If you use the couch, if you see patients four or more days a week, if you keep yourself neutral and anonymous, and if you also analyze defense and transference, then you are doing psychoanalysis. Only now is the wisdom, or the universal applicability, of some of these "technical" rules being seriously questioned.

But we are making a more serious and radical claim, namely that the whole conception of psychoanalysis as technique is wrongheaded—to borrow an epithet popular among philosophers—and needs to be rethought. Even in the so-called two-person psychologies, it relies on an assumption that one Cartesian isolated mind, the analyst, is doing something to another isolated mind, the patient, or vice versa. An earlier contribution (Stolorow and Atwood, 1992) provided extensive critique of isolated-mind assumptions in psychoanalysis. We claimed that "the development of personal experience always takes place within an ongoing intersubjective system" (p. 22).

> The intrinsic embeddedness of self-experience in intersubjective fields means that our self-esteem, our sense of personal identity, even our experience of ourselves as having distinct and enduring existence are contingent on specific sustaining relations to the human surround [p. 10].

We also argue that the instrumentalist idea of technique reduces suffering human beings to the mechanisms of classical metapsychology. This residue of positivist reductionism treats people as brains or neural networks. (Given the persistence of this residue in the larger medical mentality, it is not surprising that the first response to any problem tends to be medication, a technical response to what is seen as a mechanical problem.) A later chapter illustrates some of the effects that this technical mentality may have on a person experiencing psychotic processes.

Despite these limitations, the idea of technique is firmly, if not rigidly, embedded in psychoanalytic discourse. A recent, cogently articulated exception, however, is the work of Louis Fourcher (1996), who writes of the problems inherent in the intellectualist conception of rationality found in most psychoanalytic writing:

> A dichotomy of knower and known is established that, in turn, requires a discontinuity of knowledge and action. Knowledge is therefore related to action only unilaterally through the objectification of the therapist's activity as "technique," or through the objectification of the patient's actions as expressions of some conceptual logic or "rule" articulated by theory. Techniques are presumed to be applied according to actions or interpretations dictated by theoretically organized procedural rules [p. 524].

The concept of technique, in other words, leaves us in a Cartesian dualism with an overly intellectualized concept of interpretation. Such interpretation then comes to be contrasted with, or at least seen as separate from, the emotional understanding that inevitably forms its context and gives it meaning in the psychoanalytic situation.

THE CONCEPT OF PSYCHOANALYTIC TECHNIQUE

A review of the extensive literature—too large to describe here—on psychoanalytic technique reveals an ongoing tension between devotion to rules and insistence on flexibility. The second emphasis owes its origin to the creative pragmatism of Ferenczi, whose maxim seemed to be, "if what you're doing doesn't work, don't blame the patient; attempt to guess what is going wrong and try something else." Unfortunately, such pragmatism, with

its admission of fallibility, made Freud and many later psychoanalysts very nervous, and Ferenczi's experimental spirit was
lost to psychoanalysis until recently. Instead, most of us were
taught Freud's "rules" with a few updates. There were "parame-
ters" (Eissler, 1958), or special dispensations from the rules,[3] for
people with special disabilities that made them unable to tolerate
the rigors of orthodox psychoanalytic treatment. But these
exceptions did not bring the rules themselves into question.
Even Winnicott's importation of the spirit of child therapy did
not seriously question the concept of technique.

In fact, although Bergmann is probably correct in claiming that
psychoanalytic technique has not been a static entity and has
developed, we argue that the *concept* of technique has persisted
unchanged and continues to exert a deleterious influence in psychoanalytic thought and practice. Aside from Fourcher, we have
found few psychoanalytic authors who question the appropri-
ateness of "technique" as a significant term in psychoanalytic
discourse. On the contrary, we find conferences and journal
issues devoted to technique, and most recently Etchegoyen's
(1991) monumental and thorough compendium on the topic has
appeared.

Still, an intersubjective understanding of psychoanalysis must
question this almost universally received idea. The concept of
technique includes the idea of rules of proper and correct procedure. The primary purpose of the rules of any technique is to
induce compliance, to reduce the influence of individual subjectivity on the task at hand. Even Kohut (1971), who taught us so
much about listening to our patients, thought analysis should be
a nonidiosyncratic science that could be taught to noncharis-
matic practitioners.

While someone may point out that rules are not necessarily
bad, that they provide structure and even safety for whatever
game is being played, we must question further. Is psychoanalysis the kind of "game" or human enterprise that is primarily
capable of being played by rules? Winnicott's (1971) distinction
between *play*, which can be studied for structure and rules, and
playing, an open relational process, may be helpful here. Does

---

3. In the past, Catholics with health problems could obtain temporary dis-
pensation from fasting or from the Friday abstinence from meat.

psychoanalysis perhaps belong to the second set of possibilities, to the realm of *playing?*[4]

Before answering this question, we should consider some reasons for seeing psychoanalysis, and psychoanalytic therapy, as a set of techniques. Most obvious, and probably an important consideration that led Freud to formulate his famous "Recommendations to Physicians Practising Psychoanalysis" (1912) and boards of professional conduct to formulate their codes of ethics, is the protection of the relatively vulnerable patient. Perhaps equally prominent is the desire to protect the reputation of the profession from practitioners who lack good judgment and good personal boundaries. Neither of these reasons for placing a "frame" (Langs, 1978) around the psychoanalytic process is negligible. But we must not equate the frame with the process. Even more, we must take care to choose the frame for the particular painting, not buy the frame first and then attempt to create something or someone appropriate for it.[5]

This leads us to consider a major shortcoming in the technical approach to psychoanalysis. It amounts to assuming that the same frame will be appropriate for every patient or for each analytic couple. Intersubjectivity theory claims that

psychoanalysis seeks to illuminate phenomena that emerge within a specific psychological field constituted by the intersection of two subjectivities—that of the patient and that of the analyst. . . . [Psychoanalysis is] a science of the *intersubjective*, focused on the interplay between the differently organized subjective worlds of the observer and the observed [Atwood and Stolorow, 1984, pp. 41–42].

If this is so, then we must consider the probability that each analytic intersubjective field will develop its own process and change its own procedures as needed.

---

4. Recent papers by Lindon (1994, in press) represent a view of analysis as a nontechnical practice, freed of constraining theoretical dogma, rigidified rules, and the like.

5. This frame conception of psychoanalysis may be responsible for the ongoing discussions of analyzability or suitability for the "rigors" of psychoanalysis. In recent years, a concern for treating those previously thought unanalyzable has opened many questions of psychoanalytic theory (Kohut, 1971) and led to widespread questioning of the traditionally restrained technique or method.

The alternative is to replicate massive structures of pathological accommodation (Brandchaft, 1994) in both patient and analyst. Once again, we must remember that the purpose of rules is to induce compliance, not to facilitate the interplay of subjective worlds and perspectives, nor to support the healing of emotional pain and the opening of new developmental possibilities. Each analytic pair, or intersubjective field, must find its own process and its own frame.[6]

A related problem with technical rationality as an approach to psychoanalysis is that technique is oriented to production of a uniform product. Psychoanalysis is not producing anything but understanding, and that must be particular and individual. Technically oriented thinking blinds us to the particularity of our patients, of ourselves, and of each psychoanalytic process. Emergence may be a better concept than production—the emergence of understanding, of relatedness, of stable and positive self-experience.

Developmental studies have taught us much about the importance of flexibility and attunement between infants and caregivers. Many of us were raised in the thirties and forties, under the influence of the *Better Homes and Gardens Baby Book*, according to which babies were to be fed and diapered on a rigid schedule and left alone between the designated times. Perhaps we replicate this kind of parenting with our patients when we think and speak about psychoanalytic technique. Even for analysts who consider themselves more flexible, psychoanalytic technique, or the "frame," constitutes a kind of default setting to which to return in the face of uncertainty, and which we pass on to our students and supervisees.

The most harmful aspect of technical rationality as applied to psychoanalysis, we believe, is its attitude of knowing in advance what to expect. One of us remembers being told by a supervisor years ago that with long experience one would no longer be surprised by patients, that the incapacity for further surprise was the mark of a mature clinician. What a loss! So many possibilities of experience for patient, analyst, and analytic couple are fore-

---

6. This does not mean, as some may fear, that anything goes. We all work within the ethical and moral limits of our profession, as well as within those we have found for ourselves. We should not need rules of technique to insure ethical practice, common sense, or sound clinical judgment.

closed by devaluing surprise and new experience. Making a routine procedure out of the analytic couch, for example, ignores the developmental importance of mutual gaze regulation and other forms of facial affective communication in forming possibilities of relatedness. We must, instead, retain a thoroughly exploratory attitude toward everything we do and create together in a psychoanalysis, and relentlessly seek the meanings, both individual and cocreated.

A fallibilistic attitude toward our work and toward our patients keeps us involved in a constant effort, comparable to mutual reattunement, to experiment and to readjust. Few of us will have the experimental courage of a Ferenczi, but we need his attitude of incessant searching.

EPISTEME, TECHNE, AND PHRONESIS

The philosophical hermeneutics of Hans-Georg Gadamer provides a powerful impetus for rethinking the notion of technique, which he also criticizes under the name of method (1975b). Method, or technical rationality, is part of positivistic scientific rationality and does not belong, in his view, to interpretive understanding. Instead, he suggests, the practical reason or *phronesis* of Aristotle better describes the kind of thinking we need in the human sciences.

Aristotle distinguished three kinds of knowledge and reasoning. *Episteme*, in his view, concerns universals. It includes mathematics and the most general philosophical questions. *Techne* is the kind of knowledge concerned with production. *Phronesis*, practical reasoning or, in Gadamer's translation, "ethical know-how," always involves both the universal and the particular. In the *Nicomachean Ethics*, Aristotle's main concern was to distinguish *phronesis* from *techne*, and he did so, as Gadamer (1979) points out, in three principal ways.

First, technique can be learned and forgotten, skills can be lost. Practical reasoning, on the other hand, is an interplay between the universal and the particular, involving thoughtful and reflective choice. We are always in an "acting situation" (Gadamer's term). Second, in *phronesis*, unlike production-oriented technique, there is no prior knowledge of the right means to any end. Indeed the ends and goals themselves emerge only in the process of considering the wisest or most appropriate thing to do in this particular situation. Finally, and most important for our purposes, Gadamer (1975b) sees Aristotle's *phronesis* as a form of understanding (*synesis*). In his words,

> It appears in the fact of concern, not about myself, but about the other person. Thus it is a mode of moral judgment. . . . The question here, then, is not of a general kind of knowledge, but of its specification at a particular moment. This knowledge also is not in any sense technical knowledge or the application of such. . . . The person with understanding does not know and judge as one who stands apart and unaffected; but rather, as one united by a specific bond with the other, he thinks with the other and undergoes the situation with him [p. 288].

Instead of technique, we propose that psychoanalysis is a kind of practice in the Aristotelian sense. Practical reasoning is not concerned with the making of things without minds, but rather with relations between and among human beings. For Aristotle, practice, or practical wisdom (*phronesis*), included the realms of politics and ethics. Unlike technique, practice is always oriented to the particular. Practice embodies an attitude of inquiry, deliberation, and discovery. It eschews rules, but loves questions—questions about what is wise to do with this person, at this time, for this reason, and so on. Such wisdom can be learned, never on the basis of rules, but from the person who lives wisely. The Greeks seemed to understand that the question about the nature of wisdom could be answered fully only by pointing to the wise person.

We must ask, however, even as we grant that apprenticeship is the best psychoanalytic training, what learning it could consist in. What is this practical wisdom that we suggest as both end and means in clinical work? To answer, we must return to a basic premise or presupposition shared by Aristotle and intersubjectivity theory. *Human beings are by nature relational.* There is more to this assumption than meets the eye. It implies that our psychological life cannot be the life of the isolated mind; it must originate, grow, and change within the intersubjective contexts in which we find ourselves.

This premise requires us to ask not only what happened to this patient in what contexts of relatedness or experienced isolation to bring about the suffering he or she brings to treatment. As contextualists, we must also ask what resources for healing are available in this analyst–patient pair. We must ask how our own history, personality, and theoretical allegiances affect the understandings we reach with this patient. This is the attention to particulars that Aristotle advocated, and it does not lend itself to rules. Granted, we all have our typical ways of getting started with a patient, but these begin to modify themselves from the moment the patient walks in, or even sometimes in the initial telephone call. Practical wisdom is antimethodical and antitechnical. It is irreducibly particular and relational.

Psychoanalytic *phronesis* includes an attitude of inquiry and thoughtful reflection—Aristotle might have said "deliberation"—to indicate the attitude and process of figuring things out. It eschews the presumption that we know in advance the "false idolatry of the expert" that Gadamer finds embedded in our technology-dominated world. We might apply to psychoanalysis his more general description of a dangerous "inner longing in our society to find in science a substitute for lost orientations" (1975b, p. 318). Perhaps the worship of science and technique in the history of psychoanalysis expresses a similar longing.

Let us now consider a time-honored "technical" question from within the gestalt of practice and from the perspective of intersubjectivity theory.

SELF-DISCLOSURE AND INTERSUBJECTIVITY THEORY

Earlier we explained that the notion of practice better describes psychoanalytic clinical work than does the venerable concept of technique. We argued that although technique is appropriate in working with things without minds, where more variables can be controlled and experimentation can be replicated, practice fits work with human beings. It is no accident that we speak casually of the practice of law and medicine.[7]

---

7. Aristotle (322 BCE) believed we should also consider ethics and politics to be practices, where what is needed is not rules of technique, but the ability to deliberate wisely.

The misapplication of the concept of technique in psychoanalysis is nowhere more evident than in discussions of self-disclosure. Only by conceiving psychoanalysis primarily as an empirical science that requires rigid controls over intervening variables could we imagine that self-disclosure could be regulated by rule or precept or even by "technical recommendation." Nevertheless, generations of analytically oriented teachers and supervisors have sought to protect the process from contamination by insisting that analysts remain anonymous, just as workers at computer-chip companies don white coveralls to protect their work. Consider the famous words of Freud (1912) for whom confiding in one's patients

> achieves nothing towards the uncovering of what is unconscious to the patient. It makes him even more incapable of overcoming his deeper resistances, and in severer cases it invariably fails by encouraging the patient to be insatiable: he would like to reverse the situation, and finds the analysis of the doctor more interesting than his own. . . . The doctor should be opaque to his patients, and, like a mirror, should show them nothing but what is shown to him [p. 118].

Later analysts likewise have been concerned to protect the "pure gold" of analysis from any impurity introduced by the analyst's personality; at the same time they recognized that such complete anonymity is impossible. Greenson's story about his patient who inferred that Greenson was a liberal Democrat is illustrative. Greenson (1967) asked how the patient, a conservative Republican, had come to this conclusion.

> He then told me that whenever he said anything favorable about a Republican politician, I always asked for associations. On the other hand, whenever he said anything hostile about a Republican, I remained silent, as though in agreement. Whenever he had a kind word for Roosevelt, I said nothing. Whenever he attacked Roosevelt, I would ask who did Roosevelt remind him of, as though I was out to prove that hating Roosevelt was infantile.
> I was taken aback because I had been completely unaware of this pattern. Yet, at the moment the patient pointed it out,

I had to agree that I had done precisely that, albeit unknowingly [p. 273].

This vignette shows that prominent analysts in the ego-psychological
tradition recognized many years ago that unwitting self-disclosure
of personal data about the analyst was inevitable and that full
anonymity was impossible. Greenson's apparent chagrin, however, also illustrates the tendency of analysts to consider self-
disclosure as an unfortunate side effect of analytic work, not an
essential contributor. The patient must disclose everything; the
analyst as little as possible. Recent work in relational psychoanalysis, encouraging exploration of the patient's experience of
the analyst's subjectivity (Hoffman, 1983; Renik, 1993; Aron,
1996), has begun to remedy this one-sided view.

Intersubjectivity theory must be even more radical on this
topic. It must recognize that within any particular psychoanalytic situation (Stone, 1961) or intersubjective field, two subjective worlds are continually self-revealing and attempting to
hide. Even withholding is a form of communication. The question is what fundamental psychological convictions (emotional
organizing principles) guide the content and manner of our
revealing and hiding, both witting and unwitting, with a particular patient, and vice versa. Obviously the better-analyzed analyst will be better prepared to grapple with this question. The
well-supervised analyst or therapist from an intersubjective or
fully relational point of view will be better prepared to appreci-
ate the importance of such profound self-knowledge. We can
consider Ferenczi, who insisted on the thorough analysis of analysts, an important anticipator of intersubjectivity theory in this
respect. Not coincidentally, he was also the first to challenge the
psychoanalytic taboo on self-disclosure and to recognize that
psychoanalysis is an intimate human practice.

The question of self-disclosure, however, continues to occupy
analysts. This may mean we continue to struggle with compliance versus self-articulation (Brandchaft, 1994). Fidelity to our
ancestral legacy of psychoanalytic rules often seems a crucial
requirement for maintaining our ties with official psychoanalysis and our personal sense of identity as psychoanalysts. Reading
and hearing the history of psychoanalysis, with its many incidents of excommunication and exclusion for the crime of being
"unpsychoanalytic," makes such anxieties and conflicts more

than understandable. Conformity to the "rules of technique," which continue to cast great suspicion on any deliberate self-disclosure beyond one's carefully articulated experience of the patient, assures us, if we also conform to the other rules, that we really are analysts. In other words, the question of self-disclosure continues to be discussed, in part, because the psychoanalytic family requires of its members the suppression of spontaneity and self-expression.

But there is more. Self-disclosure of the deliberate kind remains a question because, as we mentioned earlier, psychoanalysis is a practice, not a technique. Psychoanalysis belongs to the realm of practical wisdom, not to that of techniques for the production of items or for the application of the findings of the empirical sciences, helpful and suggestive as these may sometimes be. People are not products to be shaped by techniques. Technique belongs to the realm of generality, mechanization, and routinization. The intersubjective field, on the contrary, is the realm of practice, the area of understanding, the particular interplay of particular subjectivities. This means we must address deliberate self-disclosure in psychoanalysis as a topic of serious questions and considerations. Wachtel (1993), in his textbook *Therapeutic Communication*, has made an extremely helpful start in his chapter on self-disclosure. Here let us note some important considerations that arise from an intersubjective perspective on psychoanalytic work.

Perhaps most fundamental is the question of meanings for patient and analyst. Neither disclosure nor withholding is neutral; each has a particular meaning in the context of a particular psychoanalytic treatment. Our primary concern, if we work within an intersubjective perspective, must be to understand with the patient the meanings of whatever is going on. If we believe this, then hiding our personal part in whatever is going on can only inhibit the psychoanalytic process. Of course the act of hiding, or not disclosing, will actually have a variable effect, depending on the patient's experience of this hiding, for example, as the withholding of intimate involvement, as respectfully staying out of the way, and so on. (In our next chapter we argue that there can be no neutrality in an intersubjective view of treatment.) For one patient, hearing that the analyst will be away for two weeks is more than enough. For another, there will be questions about where the analyst is going, whether the trip is business or vacation, and so on. There is no neutral way to respond. In fact, to say more to the first patient would not be neutral either.

We cannot be more specific than the intersubjective principle allows. Suppose, as we could easily be tempted to do, we considered the wisdom of an analyst's self-disclosure to depend on whether it contributes to a sense of safety, for patient, for analyst, and for the intersubjective space itself. The intersubjective field would include the intermediate or transitional area—the space of illusion and playing, the space between—so helpfully articulated and illustrated in Winnicott's work. It would also include the subjectivities of both participants. Making the whole intersubjective field increasingly safe can permit exploration, inquiry, play, and the development of new or revised psychological organization. Thus, just as patients are constantly asking themselves if it is safe to say or feel this or that with this person, analysts express their own sense of personal and intersubjective safety as we choose how or what to say or not say to a patient. The question is how—not whether—to answer a patient's inquiry, for example. If we treat emotional safety as our fundamental criterion, then we must ask how particular forms of response affect the safety of the field. There is no routine, or default, procedure. With some patients, direct response to questions followed by inquiry about meaning seems to create the safety required for deeper reflection. With others, the exact reverse seems to be true. Some ask questions hoping the analyst will ask, "Do you really want to know that?" Then a discussion ensues, not only abut the meaning of the content of the question, but even more about its function, for example, to test the analyst's ability to protect the patient from retraumatization. Some patients are thankful for this kind of response. These patients are usually those for whom intrusion and boundary violation have traumatically reduced their ability to feel safe if the other person is known to them.

But the intersubjective perspective goes further. Certain patients may need to have the experience of feeling unsafe, for example, in order to recover in the transference lost memories of traumatic endangerment. We cannot conclude that any particular intervention is better or worse without exploring its particular meaning for this particular person in the context of this particular treatment.

Let us consider a specific example, one in which a pattern of self-disclosure on the analyst's part has developed. This example differs from those recently given of what is often called countertransference disclosure.

Tim came to treatment in his late 30s, depressed and expecting to fail at everything he undertook, professional or personal, despite a history of considerable success and large talents in more than one field. Although he described his family as close, it turned out that his parents' marriage was troubled and that he had become the parentified child to several siblings. Further, his parents were both prone to rages, and Tim was frequently berated in tirades from his parents in front of friends or siblings. Nothing he could do was good enough, so explosions were always imminent. His expectation of failure was understood as closely linked to his certainty that painful and destructive humiliation was always just around the corner.

Once Tim settled into treatment and began to feel understood, a curious pattern developed. At the beginning of each session he would ask how the analyst's weekend had been, or how she was. Initially, this seemed to be just a person who had been trained to be polite and whose "structures of accommodation" (Brandchaft, 1994) were strong. So, the analyst would answer briefly, "Fine, thank you," and attempt to shift the focus to the patient's concerns. But the shift would not come easily. He would ask more, or wait for more response, before he seemed able to move on.

The analyst considered the possibility that he was, in good parentified-child style, easily recognizable through the lens of her own history of parentification, attempting to take care of her. So she continued to answer briefly, without making an issue of the ritual, and took opportunities as they arose to study with him his patterns of compulsive caregiving. While some of these began to change for him at work and at home, this approach had no effect on the beginning of sessions, so the analyst concluded she had only partially understood. She was reluctant to point out the pattern to him, imagining he would feel shamed. Yet the merely polite responses were evidently also problematic.

It seemed time to experiment. Perhaps, the analyst thought, he needed her to talk about herself to him. So, one Monday, when he asked what she had done on the weekend, she said she'd mostly done chores, had done some reading, and had been to a concert. "What was the concert?" he wanted to know. And how had the analyst liked it? After a somewhat more lengthy reply, they began to talk of his weekend, and he moved more easily into the work of the session. Since then, they have tended to "chat" for about three minutes at the beginning of each session. He has come to know a fair number of details about his analyst's interests and activities.

Now they have begun to discuss this interaction. Reflecting on the pattern they finally found together, they have concluded that he needs his analyst to be real in order to enter and stay with his own reality. If he cannot feel her as a real person with a life of her own, he feels unable to open up his own more vulnerable places. He needs to feel enough respect from his analyst to think she could trust him and talk to him. Their talking together about her interests and activities seems to make it safe for him to develop a sense of his own.

As they discussed this pattern, Tim further explained that he had always needed to check and see that the caregiver was in good emotional condition—not likely to explode—before he could venture into anything of his own, but had not realized how imperative this still felt for him. Otherwise, any indication of his own feelings and needs and concerns ran the risk of scorn and humiliation, with the consequent debilitating shame. The experiences of his adult life have only reinforced his sense of the necessity of these safety measures.

Still, to return to the earlier discussion, we do not suggest that safety, or propriety, or "the frame," or anything concrete is the ultimate criterion. From an intersubjective point of view, there is no "right answer" to questions about self-disclosure or other matters of what many call "technique." There are two people together, an analyst and a patient, trying to find understanding that will permit a reorganization of experience or perhaps a developmental second chance (Orange, 1995). Specific decisions about self-disclosures and other forms of analytic conduct need to be made on the basis of assessment as to whether their interacting meanings for patient and analyst are likely to facilitate these goals.

– 3 –

The Myth of Neutrality

The technical rationality dependent on objectivist conceptions of psychoanalysis is perhaps most evident and most harmful as expressed in the idea of analytic neutrality.

Scattered throughout our writings on the psychoanalytic situation viewed as an intersubjective system have been a number of criticisms of this idea. Here we gather together these criticisms and expand upon them, emphasizing in particular the illusory and defensive aspects of the doctrine of neutrality, as well as its intricate mythological underpinnings. We then propose an alternative analytic stance derived from intersubjective systems theory. We begin first with a critique of four conceptions of neutrality that have been prominent in the psychoanalytic literature. Two came from Freud, a third from his daughter Anna, and the last was proposed by Kohut.

Critics might object that in our portrait of the neutral analyst we set up a straw man, that critiques of, and alternatives to, the concept of neutrality already appear in the psychoanalytic literature (for example, Singer, 1977; Ehrenberg, 1992; Raphling, 1995; Renik, 1996), that relational-model (Mitchell, 1988) and constructivist (Hoffman, 1991) perspectives are already influencing analytic practice, and that only the most rigid among analysts would claim to behave in the manner we describe. Although these points may be well taken, we believe that the myth of the neutral analyst, with roots extending back through a hundred years of psychoanalytic history, continues to operate as a deeply embedded organizing principle, powerfully shaping analysts' perceptions of the analytic encounter and obscuring the intersubjective nature of the analytic process. In countless discussions with colleagues, students, and supervisees we have found that analysts

This chapter was originally published in *The Psychoanalytic Quarterly* (1997, Vol. 66, No. 3) and is reprinted here with permission.

and therapists are especially prone to make claims of neutrality when their patients' transference attributions threaten essential features of their sense of self (see Thomson, 1991). Additionally, we have found that often even relationally oriented analysts and therapists uphold neutrality as a revered, albeit unattainable ideal, deviations from which evoke shame or reactive shamelessness. It is for these reasons that we feel that a deconstructive critique of this ideal is warranted.

1. Often neutrality is equated with Freud's (1915) dictum that "treatment must be carried out in abstinence" (p. 165), typically interpreted to mean that the analyst must not offer patients any instinctual satisfactions. This technical injunction derived from the theoretical assumption that the primary constellations with which psychoanalysis is concerned are products of repressed instinctual drive derivatives. Gratification, according to this thesis, interferes with the goals of bringing the repressed instinctual wishes into consciousness, tracking their genetic origins, and ultimately achieving their renunciation and sublimation.

But in what sense can this stance of abstinence be said to be neutral? Surely not from the standpoint of the analyst who practices it, because for him or her abstinence is the expression of the deeply held belief system (some might say moral system) to which he or she adheres in conducting his or her analytic work, a system that includes basic assumptions about human nature, motivation, maturity, and psychological illness and health.

Furthermore, when one assumes a position from the *patient's* perspective, it is apparent that abstinence—the purposeful frustration of the patient's wishes and needs—could never be experienced by the patient as a neutral stance. Consistent abstinence on the part of the analyst decisively skews the therapeutic dialogue, provoking hostility and tempestuous conflicts that are more an artifact of the analyst's stance than a genuine manifestation of the patient's primary psychopathology (Wolf, 1976; Kohut, 1977). As Stone (1961) and Gill (1984) have pointed out, so-called regressive transference neuroses, thought by many to be a sine qua non of an analytic process, may actually be iatrogenic reactions to the indiscriminant application of the principle of abstinence. Thus an attitude of abstinence not only may fail to facilitate the analytic process; it may be inimical to it.

2. Closely allied to the rule of abstinence, and also considered by many to be an essential constituent of analytic neutrality, is

Freud's (1912) recommendation, consistent with his topographic theory, that the analyst "should be opaque to his patients and, like a mirror, should show them nothing but what is shown to him" (p. 118). As Gill (1984) pointed out, the assumption that the analyst can remain anonymous denies the essentially interactive nature of the analytic process. Everything the analyst does or says—including especially the interpretations offered—are products of his or her psychological organization, disclosing central aspects of the analyst's personality to the patient. These impressions, in turn, are decisive in codetermining the development of the transference. Like the rule of abstinence, analysts' misguided belief that they can keep their own personalities out of the analytic dialogue itself produces transference artifacts that may be countertherapeutic.

3. A third conception of neutrality, invoked, for example, by Kernberg (Panel, 1987), is Anna Freud's (1936) statement that the analyst "takes his stand at a point equidistant from the id, the ego and the super-ego" (p. 28), a stance that she equates with one of "clear objectivity" and an "absence of bias" (pp. 28–29). Leaving aside the considerable difficulties involved in attempting to measure distances between oneself and hypothetical mental institutions, we wish to emphasize that this concept of neutrality, like the principle of abstinence, is rooted in a value-laden theoretical belief system—the tripartite model of the mind—and hence is not unbiased or neutral at all. Interpretations offered from this metaphorical point of equidistance encourage the patient to adopt the analyst's beliefs about the structure of the mind and, to that extent, they are suggestions.

4. The myth of the neutral analyst has persisted within psychoanalytic self psychology. Reacting against the equation of neutrality with abstinent unresponsiveness, Kohut (1977) defined analytic neutrality "as the responsiveness to be expected, on an average, from persons who have devoted their life to helping others with the aid of insights obtained via the empathic immersion into their inner life" (p. 252). While we find this a felicitous characterization of an aspect of the analytic stance, we cannot agree that it describes a neutral one. Like the principles of abstinence and equidistance, it is rooted in a theoretical belief system, albeit one that places the accent on the role of emotional responsiveness in facilitating the development of the sense of self. Furthermore, as Kohut (1980) recognized, "a situation . . . in which one person

has committed himself for prolonged periods to extend his 'empathic intention' toward another" (p. 487) is surely not experienced by the patient as a neutral one, meeting as it does deep longings to be understood.

Kohut (1980), however, contended that empathy "is in essence neutral and objective" (p. 483), and Wolf (1983) has suggested that Kohut's definition of empathy "implies an attitude of objectivity with regard to the patient's subjectivity" (p. 675). To expect that an analyst can be neutral or objective with respect to a patient's subjectivity, and thereby gaze upon the patient's experience with pure and innocent eyes, is tantamount to requiring the analyst to banish his or her own psychological organization from the analytic system. This, in our view, is an impossible feat, especially when the most powerful expressions of the patient's subjectivity are directed toward the analyst—hardly a disinterested party. What analysts can and should strive for in their self-reflective efforts is awareness of their own personal organizing principles—including those enshrined in their theories—and of how these principles are unconsciously shaping their analytic understandings and interpretations.

The four variants of the myth of the neutral analyst are closely intertwined with a number of other interrelated myths that have been influential in shaping the traditional analytic stance.

THE MYTH OF INTERPRETATION WITHOUT SUGGESTION

Following Freud's (1919) distinction between "the pure gold of analysis" and "the copper of direct suggestion" (p. 168), it has traditionally been claimed that what distinguishes psychoanalysis from other forms of psychotherapy is reliance on interpretation, especially interpretation of transference, as opposed to suggestion. The dichotomy between interpretation and suggestion is closely allied with the various notions of neutrality discussed earlier, because the neutral analyst, whether from a position of abstinence, anonymity, equidistance, or empathy, is presumed to be able to offer pure interpretation without suggestion.

As Gill (1984) pointed out, "every time the analyst intervenes he may be experienced as suggesting a direction for the patient to pursue" (p. 171). We suggest that this truism vitiates the sharp distinction between interpretation of transference and suggestion. The commonly held idea that interpretation simply lifts into awareness what lies hidden within the patient is a remnant of Freud's topographic theory and archeological model for the analytic process (e.g., Freud, 1913). This model fails to take into account the contribution of the analyst's psychological organization in the framing of interpretations. Every transference interpretation—indeed, the concept of transference itself— is rooted in the theoretical framework that guides the analyst's ordering of the clinical data. Invariably, the analyst's allegiance to his or her guiding framework has roots in deeply felt personal beliefs and values (Lichtenberg, 1983; Atwood and Stolorow, 1993). Thus, each time the analyst offers an interpretation that goes beyond what the patient is consciously aware of, he or she invites the patient to see things, if ever so slightly, from the analyst's own theory-rooted perspective. To that extent, interpretations are suggestions, and it is critical to the analysis to investigate whether the patient believes he or she must adopt the analyst's viewpoint in order to maintain the therapeutic bond.

THE MYTH OF UNCONTAMINATED TRANSFERENCE

A common rationale for upholding neutrality in its various guises is the idea that noninterpretive interventions, such as gratifications or suggestions, will "contaminate" the transference so as to render it unanalyzable (Panel, 1987). The underlying assumption here is that transference can exist in a form that is "uncontaminated" by the activity of a neutral analyst. This assumption derives from the traditional conceptualization of transference, according to which the patient "displaces emotions belonging to an unconscious representation of a repressed object to a mental representation of an object of the external world" (Nunberg, 1951, p. 1). One of us (Stolorow and Lachmann, 1984/1985) has criticized this concept of transference as displacement.

The concept of transference as displacement has perpetuated the view that the patient's experience of the analytic relationship is solely a product of the patient's past and psychopathology and has not been [co]determined by the activity (or nonactivity) of the analyst. This viewpoint is consistent with Freud's archeological metaphor. In neglecting the contribution of the analyst to the transference, it contains certain pitfalls. Suppose an archeologist unknowingly dropped a wristwatch into a dig. If the assumption is made that anything found in the dig must have been there beforehand, some woefully unwarranted conclusions would be reached [p. 24].

We agree entirely with Gill's (1984) contention that "the notion that the transference can develop without contamination is an illusion" (p. 175). When transference is conceived not as displacement (or regression, or projection, or distortion), but as an expression of unconscious organizing activity (Stolorow and Lachmann, 1984/1985), then it becomes apparent that the transference is codetermined both by contributions from the analyst and the structures of meaning into which these are assimilated by the patient. Transference, in other words, is always evoked by some quality or activity of the analyst that lends itself to being interpreted by the patient according to some developmentally preformed organizing principle.

The contribution of the patient's transference to the production of the analyst's countertransference has found its place within psychoanalytic clinical theory. We are suggesting that the countertransference (broadly conceptualized as a manifestation of the analyst's organizing activity) has a decisive impact in shaping the transference. Transference and countertransference together form an intersubjective system of reciprocal mutual influence (Stolorow, Brandchaft, and Atwood, 1987). Neutral analysts, pure interpretations, uncontaminated transferences—none of these mythological entities can exist within such a system.

THE MYTH OF OBJECTIVITY

The notion of analytic neutrality supports the image of the analyst as a natural scientist making objective observations about the patient's mental mechanisms, especially the patient's transferences. Analysts embracing such an objectivist epistemology interpret from a mythological platform with a God's-eye view of the true reality that the patient's transference experiences distort. Alternatively, reverting to a doctrine of immaculate perception, some analysts claim to make direct empathic contact with the patient's psychic reality as they enter the patient's subjective world through vicarious introspection. In either case, the assumption is that the analyst can make observations, either of objective reality or of psychic reality, that are not unconsciously shaped by his or her own personal organizing principles. This myth of objectivity denies the essential indivisibility of the observer and the observed in psychoanalysis, as well as the coconstructed nature of analytic truth. From an intersubjective or perspectivalist perspective, the analyst's perceptions are intrinsically no more true than the patient's. Further, the analyst cannot directly know the psychic reality of the patient; the analyst can only approximate the patient's psychic reality from within the particularized scope of the analyst's own viewpoint (Hoffman, 1991; Stolorow and Atwood, 1992; Orange, 1995). The implication here is not that analysts should refrain from using guiding theoretical ideas to order clinical data, but that analysts must recognize the impact of their guiding frameworks in both delimiting their grasp of their patients' subjective worlds and in codetermining the course of the analytic process.

A particularly irksome example of the myth of objectivity is the analyst who pronounces a patient analyzable or unanalyzable on the basis of an "objective" assessment of the patient's personality structure and psychopathology. Analyzability, we contend, is not a property of the patient alone, but of the patient-analyst system. What must be assessed is the functioning of the system, the goodness or badness of fit between the particular patient and the particular analyst.

THE MYTH OF THE ISOLATED MIND

An objectivist epistemology envisions the mind in isolation, radically separated from an external reality that it either accurately apprehends or distorts. The image of the mind looking out on the external world is actually a heroic image or heroic myth, in that it portrays the inner essence of the person existing in a state that is disconnected from all that sustains life. This myth, pervasive in the culture of Western industrial societies, we (Stolorow and Atwood, 1992) have termed the *myth of the isolated mind* (p. 7). It appears in many guises and variations. One can discern its presence in tales of invincible persons who overcome great adversity through solitary heroic acts, in philosophical works that revolve around a conception of an isolated, monadic subject, and in psychological and psychoanalytic doctrines that focus exclusively on processes occurring within the individual person. The latter includes, for example, Freud's vision of the mind as an impersonal machine that processes endogenous drive energies, ego psychology's autonomously self-regulating ego, and Kohut's pristine self with its preprogrammed inner design. We (Stolorow and Atwood, 1992) have argued that the pervasive, reified image of the mind in isolation, in all its many guises, is a form of defensive grandiosity that serves to disavow the exquisite vulnerability that is inherent to an awareness of the embeddedness of all human experience in constitutive relational systems. All such images of the mind insulated from the constitutive impact of the surround counteract, to paraphrase Kundera (1984), what might be termed "the unbearable embeddedness of being."

The ideal of the neutral and objective analyst, impenetrable and sagelike, is just such an image, in that it disavows the deeply personal impact of the analyst's emotional engagement with patients and denies all the ways in which the analyst and his or her own psychological organization are profoundly implicated in all the phenomena he or she observes and seeks to treat. In order to dispense with the defensive invincibility and omniscience of the neutral stance, analysts must be prepared to bear the profound feelings of vulnerability and anxious uncertainty that are inevitable accompaniments of immersion in a deep analytic process. Letting go of metapsychological and epistemological absolutes and the security of standardized technique exposes analysts to the necessity of confronting the "Cartesian anxiety" (Bernstein, 1983)—their "dread of structureless chaos" (Stolorow, Atwood, and Brandchaft, 1994, epilogue).

Defensive functions similar to the ones we have been discussing played a prominent role in Freud's theory building. In our (Atwood and Stolorow, 1993) psychobiographical study of the personal, psychological origins of Freud's metapsychology, we found that Freud protected himself from awareness of the profound emotional impact of a series of early painful disappointments and betrayals by his mother by attributing his sufferings to his own omnipotent inner badness—that is, his incestuous lust and murderous hostility—a defensive translocation that found its way into his important adult relationships, including those with Fliess and with his wife, as well as into his formulations of clinical cases. This defensive solution, a form of defensive grandiosity, Freud also imported into his theory of psychosexual development and pathogenesis, a theory in which the primary pathogens were believed to be the unruly instinctual drives located deep within the interior of the psyche. In this theoretical vision, idealized images of the parents, especially the mother, were preserved, allowing Freud (1993), in a remarkable statement, to characterize the relationship between a mother and her son as "altogether the most perfect, the most free from ambivalence of all human relationships" (p. 133), and to apply the Oedipus myth in a manner that completely neglected the central role of the father's filicidal urge in setting the tragic course of events in motion. It is our belief that this same defensive principle fatefully shaped Freud's view of the psychoanalytic situation, wherein the *cordon sanitaire* that he wrapped around the parents he also wrapped around the presumptively neutral analyst, so that the patient's transference experiences could be seen as arising solely from intrapsychic mechanisms within the isolated mind of the patient, rather than being codetermined by the impact and meanings of the stance and activities of the analyst.

AN ALTERNATIVE: EMPATHIC-INTROSPECTIVE INQUIRY

If the notion of analytic neutrality is grasped as a grandiose defensive illusion to be given up and mourned, with what shall it be replaced? What is an alternative stance appropriate for the analytic situation recognized as a dyadic intersubjective system of reciprocal mutual influence, to which the organizing activities of both participants make ongoing, codetermining contributions? We (Stolorow, Brandchaft, and Atwood, 1987) have characterized this stance as one of empathic-introspective inquiry. Such inquiry seeks to illuminate the principles unconsciously organizing the patient's experience (empathy), the principles unconsciously organizing the analyst's experience (introspection), and the oscillating psychological field created by the interplay between the two (intersubjectivity). Inquiry of this kind requires continual reflection on the inevitable involvement of the analyst's own personal subjectivity and theoretical assumptions in the ongoing investigation. Unlike the posture of neutrality, the stance of empathic-introspective inquiry does not seek to avert, minimize, or disavow the impact of the analyst's psychological organization on the patient's experience. Instead, it recognizes this impact as inherent to the profoundly intersubjective nature of the analytic dialogue and seeks consistently to *analyze* it.

We are well aware that the stance of empathic-introspective inquiry, like the stance of neutrality, can serve a variety of psychological purposes for the analyst. These should be a focus of the analyst's ongoing self-reflections. (See Atwood and Stolorow, 1993, pp. 189–190, for a discussion of some personal, subjective origins of our viewpoint.) We also wish to emphasize that there is nothing in the stance of empathic-introspective inquiry that advocates denial or obfuscation of the asymmetry of the patient-analyst relationship. The meanings of this asymmetry are to be investigated, not covered over. Nor does the stance prescribe any form of emotional responsiveness, participatory enactment, or noninterpretive provision on the part of the analyst. For example, although recognizing that the analyst is constantly unwittingly revealing his or her psychological organization to the patient (Renik, 1995), the methodology of empathic-introspective inquiry does not prescribe deliberate self-disclosure by the analyst. Instead, as we explained earlier, it enjoins the analyst to make specific decisions about self-disclosures on the basis of his or her best understanding of the likely meanings of such disclosures for the patient and analyst, and on his or her assessment, arrived at with varying degrees of collaborative input from the patient, of whether such interacting meanings are likely to facilitate or obstruct the analytic process—the unfolding, exploration, illumination, and transformation of the patient's subjective world. (See Stolorow and Atwood, 1992, chapter 7, for illustrative clinical vignettes).

– 4 –

Contexts of Nonbeing
Varieties of the Experience of Personal Annihilation

We begin this chapter by briefly recounting some experiences of a young woman who had been hospitalized in a short-term treatment center during an acute psychotic episode. The patient, 24 years old at the time, suffered with multiple delusions and hallucinations that had appeared very suddenly in her life. In spite of a regime of antipsychotic medications, these manifestations persisted over a period of months. She began increasingly during this time to resist the medications, according to her later report, because of an array of side effects on her vision and muscular control of her body. The patient's psychiatrist, anxious to see improvement and bring her hospitalization to an end, decided to forcefully confront her with the seriousness of her mental illness and the importance of her complete cooperation in every aspect of her therapy. The doctor told her that she was a schizophrenic and asked her if she knew what that meant. When the patient answered that she was unsure, the psychiatrist explained that schizophrenia is a brain disease resulting from a metabolic defect rooted in genetic factors. Because of this inherited defect, her doctor continued, she would need to be taking corrective medications for the rest of her life, in the same way that a diabetic patient is required to take insulin. It was further explained that if she did not accept the reality of her illness and fully cooperate with her treatment program, she would be sent to the state hospital for long-term psychiatric care.

The impact on the patient of this confrontation, she later said, was a completely devastating one. The terms "schizophrenia" and "metabolic defect" circled through her thoughts and began to define the essence of who and what she was. As this process of psychological usurpation deepened, she felt herself being transformed into the mysterious "defect" causing her condition, as an already very tenuous sense of her own personal identity slipped away. Finally there was a paralyzing solidification—a replacement of her emotional spontaneity by an internal sensation of the inert, physical wrongness that had been ascribed to her by her psychiatrist.

In her continuing struggle with these subjective effects, the patient decided to seek some better understanding of the disease "schizophrenia" through research in the hospital library. She looked up definitions in diagnostic manuals and textbooks of psychiatry, but found nothing she could recognize or to which she could relate her experience. She wondered about the term itself—"schizo-phrenia"—about the nature of the splitting, about what exactly it was that underwent this splitting. She even read about Bleuler's (1911) seminal work introducing the term, but again could not find anything of herself in his descriptions of the separating of cognition and affectivity and of the splitting apart of the logical sequencing of thought. Finally she turned to the etymology of the word itself, tracing its roots to the original Greek. Here at last, according to her story, was something to which she could relate her own inner feelings. She said that whereas the roots of the diagnostic term are usually translated "split-mind," one could, without violence to the Greek, give the translation "torn-soul." This seemed far more apt, for she had for many years experienced herself, not as a single person, but rather as a loose collection of persons or selves that had no inner connection to one another, as if she had been somehow torn into pieces long before. She said she had a social self, a person able to get along very well with others and make them like her. She had a political self, organized around strongly left-wing attitudes. She had a sexual self that she described as enjoying sexual relations frequently and thoroughly. She had a humorous or comical self, devoted to making other people laugh. There was also a spiritual self, in which various elements of Hindu and Buddhist traditions were prominent. Each of these so-called selves had its own characteristics and its own life; the problem was that they had no relationship whatsoever to one another. She pictured them as "islands" with no land bridges between them and as "floating beings" with no common center. As a result, she further explained, she had never had any real sense of herself, no idea of who she actually was, and not even any clear picture of what she looked like.

The subjective state described by this patient was one of profound fragmentation in which the most fundamental sense of self-cohesion had been lost. This was not a case of dissociation in which different sectors of self-experience were defensively segregated as a way of avoiding otherwise intolerable conflict; it was a breakdown of the primary coherence of self-experience into a collection of subjectively unrelated "self-nuclei" (cf. Kohut, 1971) that did not coalesce around any unifying center.

Does this young woman's phenomenological translation of her psychiatrist's term for her suggest a new approach to the problem of splitting in schizophrenia, one that would place a greater emphasis on the quality of the patient's inner experience and especially self-experience? We think not, for the concept of schizophrenia is essentially a diagnostic and medical one, inextricably associated with ideas of disease process and symptomatology, and often, as well, with assumptions and hypotheses about underlying biological causation. We can nevertheless continue a psychoanalytic inquiry into self-fragmentation states, and into the broader field of self-loss experiences of which such states may be regarded as a special case. Such an inquiry covers approximately the same empirical territory that is designated by traditional psychopathology as the psychoses, but it does so from its own nonmedical, distinctively phenomenological viewpoint.

VARIETIES OF SELF-LOSS EXPERIENCE[1]

The loss of the cohesion of the sense of self may occur in one or more of three essential ways: (1) psychic fragmentation, as in the case described above, where the experience of psychological selfhood disintegrates into parts that are felt to be unrelated to each other; (2) somatic fragmentation, wherein the unity and integrity of the experience of one's body (cf. Federn, 1926) is lost, an experience often heralded by severe hypochondriasis (Stolorow and Lachmann, 1980); and (3) psychosomatic fragmentation, in

---

1. The examination of dimensions of self-experience and dimensions of self-loss was anticipated in the thinking of the late Daphne Stolorow, whose untimely death prevented her from exploring this area further.

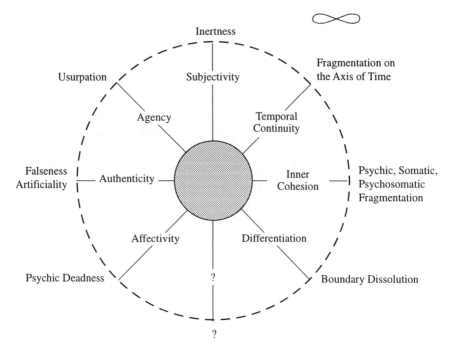

Figure 1

which one's body and mind are felt to have become irrevocably separated (Stolorow and Atwood, 1992). Inner cohesion in its different forms is actually only one of a number of aspects of self-experience in terms of which the experience of self-loss may occur. Figure 1 is a provisional representation of various of these aspects.[2]

The dimensions on which the experience of self-loss takes place include, besides inner cohesion, subjectivity, affectivity, authenticity, agency, temporal continuity, and perhaps most fundamentally, self-differentiation. What is intended in drawing these subjective states together in this way is to provide a summarized portrayal of the most extreme disturbances of the sense of self that occur in human life. The diagram is a map of psychological chaos in which attributes of ourselves that we ordinarily

---

2. Each of the lines representing a dimension of self-loss is to be understood as a bipolar continuum. The darkened area at the circle's center corresponds to organizations of experience in which the sense of self is not at issue.

take for granted are called into question or even annihilated. We are concerned here with the following kinds of experiences: disintegrating into unrelated parts; dissolving into others or diffusing into the physical environment; feeling an infinite inner deadness at the center of one's mind or soul; losing the sense of being a subject and becoming an inert, physical object; being inauthentic and unreal, a simulation lacking substance; losing possession of oneself as one's thoughts and intentions are usurped by a foreign will; and feeling such an extreme discontinuity in who one is that a fragmentation occurs along the axis of time.

The chief advantage of a conceptual scheme such as this is that it enables one to find order in the chaos as a bewilderingly diverse group of manifestations are brought together under a central conceptual umbrella. A kinship thus becomes visible between extremely varied clinical phenomena as we begin to understand our patients' delusions, hallucinations, and enactments as concretized portrayals of their experiences and struggles with these various forms of personal annihilation. One patient dons eight layers of clothing, one on top of another, in a desperate effort to rematerialize a dissolving boundary demarcating the bodily limits of her own selfhood. A second assiduously maintains a system of separate diaries, recording details of what happens each day to her various body parts, in an attempt to reunify a fragmenting sense of her body and overcome terrifying feelings of discontinuity in time. A third repeatedly cuts and burns himself in order to feel intense sensations of pain and thereby escape from an otherwise unbroken sense of inner deadness. A fourth individual cuts off all familiar relationships, changes his name, and makes a death-defying journey into the wilderness, seeking to destroy once and for all a lifetime of compliance and solidify a sense of personal authenticity and agency. A fifth patient claims she is being controlled by forces from outer space, giving symbolic form to her experience of the usurpation of her will by the agendas of other people. Although the clinical manifestations in each of these instances are very different in appearance, they all concern a struggle with the threat and/or actuality of an experience of self-loss in one or more of the dimensions described above.

Let us now consider two limitations of this schematic summary. First, any such representation in terms of a finite number of content dimensions runs the risk of becoming reified and treated as an exhaustive specification of the possibilities of human experience in this area. Subjectivity always overflows the category systems with which we try to capture it; indeed, this portrayal of variations in the experience of self-loss has displayed an unruly tendency to generate new dimensions, even as we have worked with it clinically and in teaching over the last years. It began as a threefold structure, including only cohesion, temporal continuity, and self-differentiation. But with each passing year, it seemed, clinical phenomena appeared that were not precisely covered by the dimensions previously outlined. First, it was necessary to add a dimension of affectivity or emotional vitality to cover the experiences of inner deadness so pervasively seen in this field. Then authenticity was included, addressing feelings of artificiality, of being fictional, and, in the extreme, of not existing at all. Next it was agency, designating severe disturbances of initiative, intentionality, and the will. Most recently we have recognized a need for a dimension of subjectivity, the sense of being an aware subject, alive and awake in a world felt as one's own. The loss of the sense of subjectivity becomes manifest in experiences of oneself as a lifeless, inert object or thing.

The second limitation of this conceptual scheme is that it focuses exclusively on individual experience and ignores the embeddedness of the experience of self-loss in constitutive intersubjective fields, a topic to which we now turn.

THE INTERSUBJECTIVE CONTEXT
OF SELF-LOSS

We approach the problem of defining the intersubjective fields that are associated with experiences of self-loss through a discussion of some events in the life and treatment of a young woman to whom we refer as Anna. This 20-year-old patient, who was described in detail in a previous work (Stolorow, Brandchaft, and Atwood, 1987), was preoccupied early in her therapy with achieving a state she called "becoming born." The notion of becoming born was associated with an elaborate delusional system that emerged very gradually in the analytic dialogue. She explained that she had remained silent for many weeks in order to meditate and advance the process leading to her "birth." The chief impediment to this process, according to her account, was a set of small material objects that had crystallized deep within her nervous system. These objects, which she called "blocks" and "walls," somehow obstructed the birth process and imprisoned her within the ranks of "the unborn ones." During her meditations she had tried to "dissolve" the blocks and walls, and she said that she had made tremendous progress in the work of dissolving and had brought herself to the threshold of becoming born. She made it clear she believed her analyst had himself been born and she considered him to be her "greatest birth guard."

The blocks within her were pictured as forming in the following way. Unnamed others looked at her and "rays" emerged from their eyes, traveled through space, and impacted against her face. The rays penetrated successive layers of her skin and then her skull, moving through the neural tissue until they reached the center of her brain. There they caused a mysterious solidification or crystallization, leaving a material entity called a "block" that interfered with her thoughts and arrested her "birth process."

The patient's therapist, who at first understood nothing of this imagery, was soon woven into the fabric of her delusions as she began to accuse him of "blocking" her himself and undoing the results of her work of "dissolving." Often during the analytic sessions, in what her therapist thought was an innocuous conversation about the events of Anna's day, she suddenly stared intensely at him and said, "You're blocking me, you're blocking me! Please stop! Stop it!" When the analyst reacted to her claims by asking her to explain further about what she had felt he was doing to her, she looked at him incredulously and repeated her demand that he stop. She responded to all his questions by saying, "Stop blocking me! Oh God, it's killing me! I was on the surface, but now I'm sinking, I'm dying! Going, going, going . . . gone!"

Her therapist found it increasingly difficult to sit helplessly, session after session, week after week, listening to Anna's ever-repeated pleas that he stop "blocking" her, especially when he could not identify the slightest aspect of his own behavior that corresponded to what she seemed to be experiencing. As he became more familiar with the details of her delusions, he realized she felt "rays" were flooding out of his eyes and piercing her head, but he could find no way to respond to what she said or to alleviate her pain. Finally it began to seem to him that he was being accused of committing a psychic rape and murder of his patient's brain, and he reacted to the relentless onslaught of her claims by denying that any such thing was taking place. He said he was not "blocking" her, there were no "rays" coming from his eyes, and that such things were physically impossible in any case and happened only in science fiction. Unable to comprehend her statements and demands on any level other than that of their literal concreteness, he had begun to experience her communications as an assault on his self-definition and sense of what was real. His reaction of denying the validity of her delusions was thus brought about in part by his need to reaffirm the truth of *his* convictions. Anna's response to his denials was to turn away and become mute. For several of their meetings, a pattern was followed in which, first, Anna would tell the analyst he was "blocking" her and "making walls," he would deny the reality of her claims, and then she would become silent until the session was over.

The impasse was finally broken when the therapist recognized that a profound disjunction between their respective worlds of experience had developed. The context of this recognition included not only continuing intensive work with the patient, but also concurrent developments in the analyst's self-understanding that pertained to his own early experience of loss and especially to the invalidating effects on him of certain circumstances associated with this early trauma. His new perspective enabled him to step back from the literal content of her delusional beliefs and find a different understanding of their meaning in the context of her life history. The central theme of Anna's history, as it was reconstructed in the course of her treatment, was that of invalidation: she had experienced her caregivers as invalidating her perceptions and undermining her strivings for self-delineation and autonomy throughout her development (see Stolorow, Brandchaft, and Atwood, 1987, chapter 9, for details). This history had been such as to reduce her sense of her own existence to virtually nothing, at most a fleeting shadow. As her therapist began to perceive this situation more clearly, he also saw that in order for Anna to feel that she was real and present, she required an immersion in a powerfully validating archaic selfobject bond. He recognized further that even momentary lapses in attunement to her subjective states precipitated an experience of the annihilation of her very being. The persecutory delusions regarding the blocks and walls now became intelligible in terms of Anna's struggle to protect her own psychological existence. A "block," it was understood, was a concretizing symbol of the impact on Anna of the invalidating failures of attunement of other people. It was just this devastating impact of the *analyst's* lapses that she was trying to articulate by incorporating him into the fabric of her delusional system. She experienced such failures as extreme violence against her very being, and symbolized this violence by means of the image of rays penetrating her face and depositing inert matter at the center of her brain. The buildup of the "blocking" substances concretized the transformation of her sense of inner spontaneity and subjectivity into the inertness of dead matter. The work of "dissolving" and the preparing of the way for her "birth," by contrast, symbolically represented her struggle to fight back against the violence and establish a sense of her own existence in the world as an enduring experience.

Anna's therapist now saw that his rejection of her persecutory delusions was being experienced as a new persecution, utterly foreclosing the possibility of a healing dialogue between them. When he told her there were no "rays" coming from his eyes and penetrating her brain, he was depriving her of her only means of symbolizing and communicating the destructive impact of his and others' actions on her. The denials specifically invalidated her experience of the *actual* fluctuations in his attunement to her subjective states and the corresponding fluctuations in her sense of existing. The denials also recapitulated long-standing pathogenic patterns of interaction in her history, in which she had perceived emotionally significant others as consistently rejecting her experience and pressuring her to conform to their image of who she should be.

What Anna required at this stage of her treatment was for her analyst to join her as she underwent the oscillations of being and nonbeing. When she felt the annihilating impacts of his lapses and symbolized them with the image of "blocks" forming inside her, she needed him to acknowledge the connection between what he had done (or not done) and what she was experiencing. She needed, in short, for him to understand that he and others had indeed been "blocking" her, that is, persistently failing to understand and respond to her in a way that could support her capacity to experience the steady reality of her own being. The analyst therefore stopped denying the truth of her delusional claims and began to give a new reaction to her pleas and accusations. When she cried out that he was "blocking" her and that she was "sinking" and "dying," he told her that he was deeply sorry she was experiencing something so terrible because of what he had done. He added that he wanted her to know that he had never meant to hurt her and that he hoped they could find a way to undo the damage she had suffered. As her therapist gently spoke in this way, the penetrating rays from his eyes ceased to flow. The whole delusion in fact began to recede at this point, for now Anna was able to experience her contacts with her analyst as validating acknowledgment rather than persecution, and she reacted to his new communications by feeling restored to being. This restoration, repeated many times over the next few sessions, also had dramatic effects on her other delusional ideas. The notions concerning her work of dissolving and becoming born in particular disappeared as themes in her conversation.

This patient's delusional state involved repeated experiences of being invalidated and psychologically annihilated, experiences of self-loss articulated in a language of concrete symbols that were extremely difficult for other people to understand. Some years ago, a colleague pointed out to one of us that the structure of Anna's persecutory delusion precisely reproduces the structure of the attribution that is made when a person is diagnosed as suffering from schizophrenia, seen as a medical disease.[3] In the former, rays emanated from the eyes of others, including for a period her analyst, and these rays produced a physical substance at the center of the patient's brain. In the latter, especially when strong assumptions concerning underlying biology are employed, a view of the patient is taken that imputes to his or her brain a physical defect, and major sectors of the patient's experience and conduct are then perceived as arising from this internal defect. Could Anna's delusion have initially come into being as a representation of her experience of being seen through the medical-diagnostic lens of biological psychiatry? This interpretation, while in no way rejecting biological perspectives in their own scientific and medical terms, would nevertheless highlight the importance of considering the *impact* of the use of these perspectives on the self-experience of such

---

3. We are indebted to Michael Gara for this interesting interpretation.

exceedingly vulnerable patients. Anna's experience of being viewed as suffering from a mental disease, something she consistently denied was the case, can scarcely have been other than one of extreme invalidation; for such a view inevitably "walls" the observer off from a focus on his or her constitutive impact on the patient by ascribing the patient's reactions to a pathological factor located solely inside of her.

The intersubjective field associated with experiences of self-loss and the appearance of delusions such as those expressed by Anna tend to be characterized on the one side by extreme vulnerability and a need for archaic validation, and on the other side by misunderstanding, objectification, and invalidation. When a shift occurs in this field and the patient can begin to feel the needed understanding and validation as reliably present, the annihilation experiences and the associated delusions recede and even disappear, only to return, however, when the archaic selfobject dimension of the transference becomes disrupted.

The experience of self-loss, we are suggesting, is the result of an intersubjective catastrophe in which psychologically sustaining relations to the human surround have broken down at their most basic level. It may be that the different variants of this experienced annihilation are embedded in somewhat differently organized intersubjective configurations. A configuration of special importance in this connection is one involving pathological accommodation (Brandchaft, 1993) and the extreme usurpation of agency and subjectivity, a psychological disaster that may become symbolized in the delusion of the influencing machine.

THE DELUSION OF THE INFLUENCING MACHINE

Victor Tausk, in "The Origin of the 'Influencing Machine' in Schizophrenia" (1917), characterized this delusion in the following way. The machine, operated by persecutors, is of a mystical nature, having an inner design that is only vaguely sensed. All the forces and energies known to modern technology may appear to be utilized in its malevolent activity, but the patient remains fundamentally bewildered by its precise manner of operation and the source of its inescapable powers. The machine generally works by sending out rays, waves, or other invisible emanations from its interior across space and then upon or into the patient's body, brain, or mind. Pictures, thoughts, feelings, sensations, and various motor phenomena occur that are the direct result of the machine's influence, and these are subjectively experienced as foreign to the patient and as products of someone else's will. Also, the machine may stop, block, or drain off the patient's own thoughts and emotions, and all of these effects tend to be felt as involving electrical, magnetic, or directly mechanical forces applied to the patient's head or body as a whole.

Perhaps the most important contribution of Tausk's original article lies in his formulation of the phenomenology of psychosis as centrally involving what he called "loss of ego boundaries"—in the language of the current presentation, the experience of boundary dissolution or self-loss on the dimension of self-differentiation. A common manifestation to which Tausk points as an example is the complaint that everyone knows the patient's thoughts, that these thoughts are not enclosed in the patient's head, but are somehow spread throughout the world and occur simultaneously in the heads of all persons. Curiously, his main interpretation of the psychological origins of the delusion of the influencing machine appears to be inconsistent with this formulation. Tausk analyzes the genesis of this delusion into essentially three stages. First, the patient feels disturbing sensations of inner change, both psychological and physical, but without any thought of these having any special originator. Second, the inner changes are psychologically rejected and increasingly felt as alien, and an originator somehow contained within the patient's own boundaries begins to be imagined. Third and last, a sense of persecution arises as the disturbing inner alteration is projected on to the outer world and attributed to a foreign hostile power making use of the influencing machine. The image of the machine itself, according to Tausk, is produced by a projection outward of a pathologically regressed experience of the patient's whole body, identified with the male genital. The notion that the machine is identified with the male genital, or that the projected body carries that identification, appears to have been influenced by Freud's (1900) discussion of machine imagery in dreams, in which it was argued that such imagery is invariably a matter of phallic symbolism. Consistent with the classical psychoanalytic viewpoint, Tausk's analysis is exclusively intrapsychic, tracing the machine and its influences to internal conflicts within the patient's own mind.

The defense of projection, which figures centrally in Tausk's analysis, involves a translocation of psychological attributes from the self to others or to the world experienced as outside of oneself, and thus presupposes a stable boundary demarcating the limits of one's selfhood. The essence of projection is the attribution of the disowned to the realm of the "not-I"; if what is "I" and what is "not-I" have no stable boundary defining and separating their distinctive provinces, it makes little sense to speak of a projection from one to the other. In addition, it has been our clinical experience that the influencing machine has no stable location in subjective space. It may be here, there, or anywhere, within or without, perhaps everywhere; for that matter, space itself, in the psychological states wherein these phenomena occur, has no stable geometry and certainly no clear delineation of personal selfhood. Consistent with Tausk's description of the loss of ego boundaries, the machine is always *both* inside and outside; for the "influences" always play directly upon the interior of the body or brain, most often upon the patient's very thoughts. What is relatively stable in these experiences, however, is the patient's experience of being influenced, the sense of a will being at work that is not the patient's own. In interpreting the experience of the machine's influences as a projection, Tausk confuses and confounds the experience of *subjective locus* (inside or outside) with the experience of *foreignness*. In this respect, he follows the example set by Freud (1911) in the Schreber case, wherein Schreber's experience of certain of his own thoughts as absolutely foreign to him was interpreted as a product of projection. The thoughts were about how exquisitely pleasurable it would be as a woman to "succumb to sexual intercourse," and they represented the first step in the formation of an elaborate delusional system. In his *Memoirs*, Schreber describes how such ideas could not be his own and must somehow have been induced in him by persecutory, perhaps telepathic influences from someone. This experience of the foreignness of a thought occurring in Schreber's mind Freud attributed to a defensive disowning and projection of an underlying homosexual impulse that fundamentally, if unconsciously, was Schreber's own. Thus Schreber's paranoid state of feeling persecuted and influenced was ultimately explained as a defensive transformation of intrapsychic tensions and conflicts. Schreber eventually went on to develop the idea that he was the target of a campaign orchestrated by God to murder his soul and transform him into a woman. The image of God that emerges in Schreber's delusional world resembles nothing so much as an immense machine, existing somehow at the origin and center of the universe, and sending out "rays" that penetrate Schreber's personal being and produce all manner of changes (called "miracles") in his mind and his body. Whereas Freud traced this delusion to Schreber's unconscious homosexual tie to his father, more recent scholarship (e.g., Schatzman, 1973; Niederland, 1984; Orange, 1995) has presented persuasive evidence and compelling arguments that the persecutory delusions in this case depict a primary persecutory reality inhering in Schreber's having been forced as a child to surrender passively to the autocratic, extremely bizarre child-rearing practices of his father. The essence of being a woman, for Schreber, was the attitude of passivity and compliant surrender to the will of the other. His thought about how pleasurable it would be to succumb to sexual intercourse as a woman therefore may be understood as encapsulating the passive compliance that was his father's absolute condition for having any connection with him. One can thus see that this thought, far from embodying any authentic sexual desire of Schreber's own (consciously or unconsciously), expresses in a sexual*ized* but unequivocal language the sacrificial delivering up of his sense of personal agency in "succumbing" to the all-defining agenda and will of his father.

The delusion of the influencing machine, regarded from an intersubjective viewpoint, represents first of all a concretization of the experience of the loss of agency. The essential quality of the influences emanating from the machine is that they bring about changes in the patient's mind or body completely independently of his or her initiative. The continuity of the operation of the patient's own intentionality is thus disrupted as the mind and body become subject to an alien will. The primary event in the intersubjective field of this delusion, as we have come to understand it, is an extreme pathological accommodation, accompanied by a destabilization of the patient's experience of selfhood. The sense of agency has been compromised by the substitution of an agenda lying outside the patient's personal volition, and this experience is symbolized by the image of influences radiating from a physical object into the self. Consistent with some of Tausk's observations, we have encountered a number of instances in which the machine is pictured as having a clearly phallic shape and the influence visualized in imagery suggestive of sexual penetration. It is our belief that the sexual imagery is here being drawn upon to represent primarily a rape of the mind rather than of the body. One of us worked with a patient some years ago who provided a dramatic example of such sexual symbolism. This patient, a 60-year-old woman, was brought to a psychiatric hospital following her attempt to break into the home of Harry Truman, the former president of the United States, then living in Independence, Missouri. When asked why she had tried to enter Truman's home, she answered, "Truman has my head! He stole my head, I want my head!" After it was gently pointed out to her that her head was exactly where it should be and had not been taken from her, she screamed, "Truman! Truman!" The patient further explained that the former president had entered into a conspiracy against her with the Con-Edison Company of New York, and that enormous tube-shaped machines had been constructed in an effort to destroy her. These machines, described only as massive cylindrical objects, had been placed in some hidden location and generated "yellow rays" that emanated from their tips. The rays crossed space, according to her description, and flowed directly into her vagina. Then the energy of the rays slowly traveled up through her body into her throat, where they caused a "small man" to materialize, an entity that periodically assumed control of her voice. Her speech was often interrupted by incomprehensible cursing and shouting, and she attributed the interruptions to "the man in my throat." These delusions vividly symbolize the process of psychological usurpation: first, in the image of the stealing of her head; and second, in the experience of her voice being taken over by the man who had materialized in her throat. The incorporation of Harry Truman into the persecutory delusion appeared to be in part related to the ex-president's name: Truman, True-Man, the Man with the Truth, the Truth to which one must surrender one's own mind. The specifically sexual imagery in this case, in which the phallic machines emit rays that penetrate the patient's vagina, symbolically captured the patient's experience of compliantly "succumbing" (Schreber) to an invasively powerful masculine will.

Two questions may be posed regarding the conditions under which the delusion of the influencing machine crystallizes. First, why does the experience of being influenced by others in pathological accommodation become concretized in a delusional form in the first place? We answer that the formation of delusions tends to occur in a context of radical invalidation, wherein the individual's sense that his or her perceptions and feelings have any validity whatsoever is dissolving and becoming lost (Stolorow, Brandchaft, and Atwood, 1987). The delusion, by casting the dissolving experience in a tangible, concrete form, expresses an effort to hold on to a reality that is in the process of slipping away. In this connection, our view contrasts sharply with that of classical Freudian theory, according to which a delusion forms in consequence of a person's turning away from an external reality that has become too painful or a source of intolerable conflict.

The second question to be answered is: Why does the concretization of psychological usurpation take the specific form of becoming victim to the influences of a *machine*? A machine strikes us the antithesis of subjectivity and as an apt symbol for the experience of the eradication of one's sense of oneself as an active agent and subject. The intrusion into one's inmost thoughts and feelings of mechanically regulated qualities implies the annihilation of subjectivity, the disappearance of emotional spontaneity, and the replacement of the sense of creativity and unpredictability by the dead workings of a physical device. In coming under the power of such a device, we would point out, one becomes its extension and thus a machine oneself.

The intersubjective context of the delusion of the influencing machine is one of extreme pathological accommodation and involves the substitution of a foreign agenda for the person's own spontaneous desire and initiative. In becoming captive to another person's will, one loses not only freedom of action but also freedom of thought, imagination, and feeling. Also characteristic of this context, as we have observed it, is that the domination of the other is itself hidden from view, so any and every negative reaction to the invasive captivity becomes an inexplicable eruption, perhaps reflecting something deeply flawed within oneself. As the sense of agency undergoes a spreading, deepening annihilation, the image of a machine appears, condensing the alien power in whose paralyzing grip one finds oneself into the picture of a deadly physical object. By crystallizing the source of the usurping power of the other into a specific, tangible machine, the patient concretizes, encapsulates, and thus attempts to localize a pressure otherwise felt as pervading his or her entire subjective universe. The focus on the image of a machine may additionally provide an illusory sense of the possibility of the recovery of agency, for any such tangible object existing in the world can at least in theory be found, turned off, or destroyed.

DEFECTS IN THE SELF[4]

As a further example of the new understandings that become possible through inquiry into the intersubjective context of the experience of self-loss, we now take up the self-psychological doctrine of defects in the self. Our discussion again begins with a description of a young woman, one whose experiences and delusions bear interestingly on this doctrine. This woman, a 22-year-old, hospitalized psychiatric patient, said that she had no self, was not real, did not exist, and was absent rather than present. The defect in her self, speaking phenomenologically, was not located in a preconscious "sense of the incomplete reality of the self" (Kohut, 1971, p. 210), which has been described as the core of narcissistic personality disorders; her experience was rather one involving *a conscious sense of the complete unreality of herself.*

The clinical context of her therapist's early encounters with this patient involved a struggle over a program of self-starvation she had undertaken. She had refused all food for a period of many days and her weight, already low at the outset of this adventure, had begun to diminish to an alarming degree. In discussions she explained that she could not partake of food because anything she ate would necessarily be taken from someone else. It also concerned her greatly that animals and plants had to be sacrificed in order that she have something to eat. She said that she was made of "pure love" and thus could not do anything to deprive or bring harm to other living beings. The notion that she might die from her starvation seemed to have no meaning to her and she was impervious to all rational argument concerning her diet.

---

4. We wish to thank Bernard Brandchaft, whose insights into the limitations of self-psychological conceptualizations of early pathological organizations of experience inspired this section of this chapter. He also reviewed an early draft of the material dealing with the concept of self-defects and made a number of valuable suggestions that have been incorporated into the final text.

Her therapist's initial approach to this patient was extremely concrete, emerging from a wish to stop her from killing herself rather than from any real understanding of what she was enacting. He told her that it was absolutely vital that she begin to eat again and that he had arrived at a solution he was sure she would find acceptable. He brought plastic bags of fresh fruit, nuts, and raisins to their daily sessions and told her that all the fruit and nuts had fallen spontaneously from trees into special baskets laid beneath the branches. Everything she was to eat would otherwise have simply gone into the ground and so she was free to partake of this nourishment without worrying about causing harm to others. He tried to show a sparkle of humor in his eyes as he presented this, in case the patient decided to focus on the total preposterousness of what he was telling her. Her reaction, however, was one of apparent acceptance and she began to eat what he had brought. Her psychiatrist later joined in this intervention by taking cans of breakfast drink, denting them with a hammer, and presenting them to the patient with the explanation that they had been retrieved from the garbage. These too she began to accept. Over a period of weeks, again for reasons her therapist did not understand, the issue of self-starvation and the idea of being made purely of love receded from the patient's conversation and finally disappeared. In the meantime she continued to accept the things her therapist brought to her, the breakfast drinks, and a gradually increasing number of other foods from the hospital cafeteria.

Some months later the patient and her therapist were walking across the hospital grounds to the canteen for coffee and doughnuts. She turned to him and made the following statement. "There is this huge machine. Someone's inside it hooked in. Wires come out of the machine and are hooked into another person. There is a switch on the machine and it has only two settings. When it is switched on one setting it makes you forget all your memories and even your own name; when it is switched on the other one, it electrocutes the other person."

This remarkable machine concretizes an organizing principle according to which the survival of other persons is contingent on the cancellation of the experience of one's own authentic selfhood. If the patient retains her own memories, thoughts, and identity (symbolized by her name), someone else dies; if that other person lives, she loses all sense of herself. A partial isomorphism exists between this delusional machine and the starvation project described earlier. In the starvation enactment, if she ingested food and lived, others would have been harmed or made to die; if others were to be protected, her life would necessarily have been sacrificed. The embracing of love as her identity can be compared to the switch on the machine being set in the position that protects other persons at her expense. In a universe with these and only these possibilities—to live but to kill, or to love but to die—she had opted for love.

Adopting the doctrine of defects in the self creates a clinical perspective from which our focus is on what is missing in the experiences we seek to understand, rather than on what is present. In exploring our patients' worlds we are guided by an image of an optimally structuralized self, felt as cohesive in space, continuous in time, and with a stable sense of self-esteem. Disparities between what is presented to us and this image are then viewed as reflecting self-defects, results of various kinds of developmental deficits and arrests. Seeing the patient we have been describing from this viewpoint, as indeed her therapist did in their early work together, one's focus would tend to be on her sense of nonexistence, on the apparent absence of a cohesive and temporally continuous self, and one would be inclined to attribute this absence to an internal structural deficiency arising out of her developmental history. What such a view could fail to bring into focus, however, is that her experiences of nonbeing were themselves embedded in a well-consolidated structure of experience, an organizing principle according to which life affords only the mutually exclusive alternatives of others being murdered or of undergoing psychic death oneself. This structure, as it was reconstructed in the course of the patient's treatment, appeared to have arisen out of a mergerlike closeness with her father that provided the only consistent tie during most of her developmental years, a closeness serving to protect the father from otherwise devastating feelings of worthlessness and suicidal depression. As the treatment proceeded, she expressed intimations of a developing sense of existing in her own right in a transitory delusion of having been attacked and stung by a swarm of bees. Her therapist came to understand these stinging bees as concretized symbols of sporadic moments of painfully felt being ("bees") interrupting the deathlike emotional numbness that had previously pervaded all her experiences. The delusion of the bees may also have carried a continuing trace of the machine, in that her increasing shift from selflessness toward a disenmeshed position honoring her own spontaneous desire in the context of the new attachment to her therapist would inevitably be accompanied by a sense of deep foreboding and endangerment. Perhaps the painful sting of the bees corresponds to the "zap" of the machine that obliterates all of one's memories and identity. The steps of growing authenticity were also associated at every stage with consuming anxiety for the well-being of her therapist, expressing again the close link in her world between existing as her own person and endangering emotionally important others.

This case lends itself to a highlighting of the very different conceptions of psychic structure that appear in self psychology and intersubjectivity theory. In the original formulations of self psychology, Kohut (1971) envisioned psychic structure in terms of a reified conception of the self. The self, instead of being seen solely as an individual's intersubjectively constituted experience of his or her own personhood—his or her sense of "I-ness" or "I-experience" (Jones, 1995)—was viewed as a mental entity in its own right, achieving through processes of (transmuting) internalization varying degrees of its own internal structuralization. The concept of structure within intersubjectivity theory, by contrast, refers to broad patterns within which experience repeatedly takes form, prereflective organizing principles manifest as recurring themes in the flow of subjective life (Stolorow, 1978). If we dispense with the reifications inhering in traditional self-psychological formulations and rely instead on the idea of organizing principles, then we can see that the experiences of nonbeing and of unreality present in our clinical case are not the result of any deficiency or lack of structure. These experiences arise as the product of a quite specific psychological structure, namely, the organizing principle according to which the survival of the other is contingent on the cancellation of the sense of one's own authentic existence.

In some earlier writings critiquing classical metapsychology (Atwood and Stolorow, 1980, 1993), we argued that many of the reified constructs in psychoanalytic theory can be profitably understood as condensed symbols of various classes of experiences and can therefore be retranslated into phenomenological terms. Applying this translation project to the topic of the present discussion, the question arises: What are the experiences reified in the notion of defects in the self? We believe there are two groups of such experiences, each associated with a distinctive intersubjective context of origin. In one of these, self-experience is dominated by a sense of defectiveness, of being inherently flawed, perhaps of lacking something essential that a complete person should certainly have. An intersubjective context producing this theme is one in which bonds to caregivers are repeatedly disrupted but the child maintains a tenuous sense of connection by shamefully ascribing the disruptions, or the child's painful emotional reactions to them, or both to a weakness, flaw, or defect within himself or herself. The second group of experiences are ones in which the individual feels a diminished sense of existing at all, a deficiency in experience of the person's very being. This is illustrated in the extreme by the case presented earlier. A common intersubjective context of origin for this pattern of self-experience involves very profound invalidation and the association of authenticity with the danger of the total loss or obliteration of emotionally important others.

The vision of the self as a reified structure needing nutriment from selfobjects, as noted earlier, establishes a clinical focus on what is missing rather than on what is present in self-experience. This focus seriously circumscribes our observational range as it leads to the homogenization and reduction of the multiple dimensions of transference to an overinflated selfobject aspect (Stolorow, 1995). It has become apparent to us, for example, that the term *selfobject transference* is being used to refer to two types of relational experiences that have distinctly different origins and meanings. In one, the patient longs for the bond with the analyst to supply missing developmental experiences—what Kohut originally meant by selfobject transferences. In the other, the patient seeks responses from the analyst that would counteract invariant organizing principles that are manifestations of what we (Stolorow, Brandchaft, and Atwood, 1987) call the repetitive dimension of the transference. In the former, the patient longs for something missing; in the latter, the patient seeks an antidote to something crushingly present. Making this distinction has profound implications for the framing of transference interpretations, whereas merging the two types of relational experience into an overinclusive selfobject concept obscures Kohut's clinical contribution. One's interpretive approach to a patient's wishes for mirroring, for example, will be radically different, depending on whether the patient seeks mirroring of an emerging, long-sequestered expansiveness or of a defensive grandiosity serving as an antidote to an underlying sense of defectiveness or deficiency (Morrison and Stolorow, 1997). In the case of the former, mirroring experiences foster integration and developmental transformation; in the latter, addiction to the analyst's "responsiveness." It is the search for antidotes to crushing organizing principles, not for archaic selfobject functions, that leads to such clinical phenomena as addictions, sexual perversions, and aggressive, grandiose enactments.

CONCLUSION

The foregoing represents a contextualist view of experiences of nonbeing in several respects. First, it deabsolutizes and dereifies what organized medicine calls the "psychoses" and restores to the phenomena of self-loss, disintegration, and nonbeing their experiential character. Second, the "map of psychological chaos" provides a way to orient ourselves among these experiences of personal annihilation by bringing apparently diverse clinical phenomena together under a single conceptual umbrella. Third, we have described the intersubjective contexts in which the experience of self-loss occurs, emphasizing how invalidation, compliance, and objectification are expressed in specific forms of psychological disintegration. A contextualist understanding of the intersubjective origins of these experiences can lead the clinician to imagine creative possibilities for transforming systems of personal and relational devastation. The exploration of such possibilities of psychotherapeutic intervention represents, in our view, one of the most important areas of continuing clinical psychoanalytic research.

– 5 –

Thinking and Working Contextually

> To study the word as such, ignoring the impulse that reaches out beyond it, is just as senseless as to study psychological experience outside the context of that real life toward which it was directed and by which it is determined.
>
> —Mikhail Bakhtin
> *Discourse in the Novel*

The book *Contexts of Being* (Stolorow and Atwood, 1992), called attention to the importance of seeing such fundamentals as mind, unconscious, and mind-body relations in their formative and ongoing intersubjective contexts. Isolated mind psychology, it was claimed, "ignores the constitutive role of the relationship to the other in a person's having any experience at all" (p. 9). Psychological phenomena such as trauma, pathology, and fantasy were examined in the developmental and relational contexts that give them ongoing life. Finally, what we might now call contextualist thinking was applied to clinical problems like therapeutic alliances and impasses.

We must emphasize, because we are often misunderstood on this point, that the intersubjective viewpoint does *not* eliminate psychoanalysis's traditional focus on the intrapsychic. Rather, it *contextualizes* the intrapsychic. The problem with classical theory was not its focus on the intrapsychic, but its inability to recognize that the intrapsychic world, as it forms and evolves within a nexus of living systems, is profoundly context-dependent. In *Contexts of Being* this issue was addressed as follows:

> The concept of an intersubjective system brings to focus *both* the individual's world of inner experience *and* its embeddedness with other such worlds in a continual flow of reciprocal mutual influence. In this vision, the gap between the intrapsychic and interpersonal realms is closed, and, indeed, the old dichotomy between them is rendered obsolete [p. 18].

Pushing this line of argument even further, we contend that from an intersubjective systems perspective, the very distinction between one-person and two-person psychologies—at the heart of much current debate in psychoanalysis—is obsolete, because the individual and his or her intrapsychic world are included as a subsystem within the more encompassing relational or intersubjective suprasystem (Stolorow, in press). The very idea of a two-person psychology continues to embody an atomistic, isolated-mind philosophy in that two separated minds (the "windowless monads" of the philosopher Leibniz) are seen to bump into each other. Such a conception fails to recognize the constitutive role of relatedness in the making of all experience. We ought to speak instead of a contextual psychology.

Intersubjectivity theory differs from other psychoanalytic theories in that it does not posit particular psychological contents that are presumed to be universally salient in personality development and in pathogenesis. It is a process theory offering broad methodological and epistemological principles for investigating and comprehending the intersubjective contexts in which psychological phenomena, including psychoanalytic theories, arise. It also provides a framework for integrating different psychoanalytic theories by contextualizing them. From an intersubjective perspective, the content themes of various metapsychological doctrines—Freud's Oedipus complex, Klein's paranoid/schizoid and depressive positions, Kohut's mirroring, idealizing, and twinship longings, and the like—can be deabsolutized, deuniversalized, and recognized as powerful metaphors and imagery that can become salient in the subjective worlds of *some* people under particular intersubjective circumstances. Personal experience is pictured here as fluid, multidimensional, and exquisitely context-sensitive, with multiple dimensions of experience oscillating between figure and ground, within an ongoing intersubjective system of reciprocal mutual influence.

Now, however, we wish to raise a somewhat different question. If, as we have sometimes stated and continually implied, to think and work from our intersubjective perspective means thinking and working as contextualists, we must ask what it could mean to think contextually. Let us first approach the question itself contextually, that is, in terms of one sort of context— the historical.

FROM ISOLATION TO CONTEXT

From the time of Descartes, whose own historical context included the Copernican revolution and the condemnation of Galileo, the dominant intellectual ideal of Western thought has been the quest for purity and certainty. In Descartes' own words, we needed to be able to rely on "clear and distinct ideas." The way to purity and certainty, to clarity and distinctness, was to isolate whatever was being studied. Today we would speak of reducing the influence of contaminating variables. Descartes' method was systematic doubt, carried on by an isolated individual, by a "windowless monad." If he could reject everything he could possibly doubt, what remained would constitute a reliable foundation for all knowledge. Watching Descartes' thought-experiment, we can see with Cartesian clarity how much the standpoint of the observer influences the observations that are made and the conclusions that are reached. An isolated observer finds an isolated mind. Similarly, Locke's empiricism created what Taylor (1989) calls "the punctual self" (p. 160), or the disengaged self. The atomism of modern epistemology, whose consequences for psychoanalytic thinking one of us has previously noted (Orange, 1995), is a consequence of Cartesian and Lockean isolation. The modern self is an individual, isolated from relatedness and community, devoted to technical rationality and, in its Romantic variation, to a sensed oneness with the natural world.

Similarly, empiricists like Hume saw isolated bits of sense-data as the only components of knowledge, and isolated moments as reducing to illusion any integrity of personal identity or self-experience. In contemporary psychoanalytic thought we can see similar tendencies reappearing in the preoccupation with personal multiplicity (Bromberg, 1996; Harris, 1996; Flax, 1996). We must ask ourselves whether different aspects necessarily entail no significant unity or integrity. As the medieval philosophers (Wuellner, 1956) taught us, there are different kinds of distinctions to be made. These include (1) "real distinctions" between entities thought to be actually divisible, (2) "distinctions of reason" or logical distinctions between realities not divisible except by words or names, entities without real plurality, and (3) distinctions of reason with a basis in reality, sometimes known as virtual distinctions (e.g., between mind and body or between the infinity and perfection of God). We ought to ask whether the multiplicities currently fashionable refer to entities really distinct from one another, or to aspects of beings temporarily experienced or named as distinct. If the latter, how do we conceive the underlying unity? If the former, how do we conceive human agency and responsibility when we view people as irreducibly multiple? Granted, not every aspect of a person—even a philosophically inclined person—takes any interest in this question. Still, supposing someone does, who is that someone? That "I" is a person who, in some temporal and relational contexts, experiences herself or himself as interested in philosophical questions. The point, for a psychoanalyst, is to take an interest in the relational and intrapsychic contexts that give rise to particular configurations of self-experience. We do assume an ontological continuity and unity of the person, whose experience, however, may be one of discontinuity or continuity, multiplicity or unity. We cannot assume, with Hume and other atomists (cf. Taylor, 1985), that there *can* be no continuity of I-experience. Without awareness that there are several kinds of distinctions, a useful attention to multiple aspects of experience and of relatedness may degenerate into atomism, or may be seen as incompatible with an organized sense of personal continuity.

The work of Hegel (1807) may have been the first significant attempt to overcome the atomist presuppositions of modern thought. Hegel's dialectics saw all phenomena as embedded in larger historical and intellectual contexts. His analysis of the master-slave relationship, which upended and recontextualized forever our thinking about dominance relations, is a famous example. But Hegel's universalizing *Geist* was misunderstood to justify other forms of oppression, so his thought has remained underemployed as a challenge to the atomism of modern philosophy.

Other sources, however, have supported the development of our contextualist thinking. These are phenomenology, Gestalt theory, Mannheim's sociology of knowledge, Tomkins's ideas on the psychology of knowledge, the ontological hermeneutics of Gadamer, and the contextualist philosophies of Bakhtin, of the deconstructionists, and especially of Wittgenstein. Let us look briefly at the contribution each has made.

Phenomenology, as recognized in *Structures of Subjectivity* (Atwood and Stolorow, 1984) and in *Emotional Understanding* (Orange, 1995), points both philosophical and psychoanalytic inquiry toward the experience of the subject. Paradoxically, however, the phenomenological method of bracketing assumptions, thereby decontextualizing experience, draws attention to those very preconceptions—we call them organizing principles—in which all experience is inextricably embedded. The failure of Husserl's effort to reach pure subjectivity has led us instead to our realization of the centrality of a thoroughly contextualized subjectivity. Such subjectivity, phenomenologists now understand, can only be the experience of a historically situated subject. To be a subject is to be positioned in the intersubjective contexts of past, present, and future. The phenomenological reduction is thus transformed into a phenomenological elaboration of complexity and process as properties of larger relational systems. Unremitting focus on the organization of personal experience, eschewing all isolated, reified mental entities, unveils the inescapable embeddedness of personal experience in constitutive intersubjective fields.

Gestalt psychology forms a second intellectual source for contextualist ideas. It is easy to forget what a radical idea it is to think of all perception as determined by surroundings. Not only must we reject the isolated mind as knower and experiencer, we must consider that nothing can be known or experienced apart from the context in which it appears. The very being of much, if not all, of what we know is constituted by context. Psychological phenomena receive both existence and meaning from context. Context determines the foreground-background shifting to which we attend in our analysis of transference (Stolorow, Brandchaft, and Atwood, 1987). Gestalt psychology accords well with perspectivalist thinking (Orange, 1995), according to which there are an indefinite number of perspectives on any reality. The Rashomon effect, as in "The Blind Men and the Elephant," where different observers see very different stories or versions of an event, results from the recontextualizing effect of shifting perspectives.

Mannheim's (1936) sociology of knowledge and Tomkins's ideas on the psychology of knowledge (Atwood and Tomkins, 1976) contributed heavily to our early awareness of the contextual origins of ideas, in particular the psychoanalytic theories whose subjective origins were explored in *Faces in a Cloud* (Atwood and Stolorow, 1993). Mannheim's sociology of knowledge, as noted in *Faces*, "views intellectual phenomena in the formative social and historical setting of their origin and investigates the dependence of thought upon its social milieu" (p. 12). It insists that knowledge is always context-dependent. Similarly, Tomkins's (1963, 1991) studies of the relation of affective experience to systems of knowledge taught us to examine the contexts of emotional development that color and influence psychoanalytic ideas.

Philosophical hermeneutics, especially the work of Hans-Georg Gadamer (1975a,b; Orange, 1995), forms another source of our contextualist thinking. The fabric of preconceptions that Gadamer calls "prejudice" and the historical matrix he calls "tradition" constitute the context for all interpretation and understanding. There is no understanding in isolation.[1] Similarly, in psychoanalysis, there is no isolated mind, no isolated meaning, no isolated anything. Interpretation is conversation, understanding is making sense together, and whatever is understood or interpreted exists in relational and historical networks. We understand only from within the context and perspective of tradition. We understand psychoanalytically only from a relational perspective, from within a specific intersubjective system. Psychoanalytic meanings are always cocreated and codetermined.

In addition, the later philosophy of Ludwig Wittgenstein (1953) brings a pragmatic (*not* instrumentalist) contextualism to our thinking. His famous dictum, "The meaning is the use,"

---

1. Sometimes postmodern thought is misunderstood to claim that the existence of intellectual presuppositions automatically invalidates whatever idea is thus contextualized. In our view, Putnam is correct in saying that "the fact that an interpretation presupposes a view is deplorable only if the view is deplorable" (Putnam, 1990, p. 130).

points away from meaning and interpretation in isolation toward a thoroughly and radically contextualist view of meaning. In his later writings and conversations Wittgenstein examined, almost obsessively, the meaning particular expressions could have within what he called "language-games." A language-game (*Sprachspiel*) was a system of meaning that gave sense, like a gestalt, to the things that could be said within it. No expression could have meaning in isolation, apart from its context or language-game. The language-game itself belonged to a larger context of a *Lebensform*, or form of life. By *Lebensform*, Wittgenstein (1953) probably meant (cf. Carver, 1994) the distinctively human form of life that includes mastery of languages. "Can only those hope who can talk? Only those who have mastered the use of language. That is to say, the phenomena of hope are modes of this complicated form of life" (p. 174).

Belatedly, we and others in the Western world have become aware of the dialogic contextualism of Mikhail Bakhtin. His idea that we all speak many languages, each of which is a perspective on the world, resembles Wittgenstein's.[2] It differs, however, in Bakhtin's lesser attention to the rule-governed internal coherence of languages, and his greater emphasis on dialogue among languages. The words most associated with his work—much of it in literary criticism—are dialogue and *heteroglossia*. By the latter he seems to have meant the multiplicity of potential meanings in any utterance—that each word and expression belongs to the particular language of a particular speaker in a particular dialogic context—"there are no 'neutral' words and forms" (Bakhtin, 1981). "Each word tastes of the context and contexts in which it has lived its socially charged life; all words and forms are populated by intentions. Contextual overtones are inevitable in the word" (p. 293).

Another prominent source of contextualist thinking appears in the deconstructionist critique offered by "postmodern" thinkers who identify and attack foundationalism, objectivism, and isolated-mind ontologies in all their many guises. Indeed, as Barratt (1993) points out, psychoanalysis can itself be seen as a decon-

---

2. Bakhtin's brother Nicholai had a long series of conversations with Wittgenstein that may have supported the turn from the logical empiricism of the *Tractatus Logico-Philosophicus* (Wittgenstein, 1921) toward the contextualism of the *Philosophical Investigations* (Monk, 1990).

structive identification and critique of unconsciously held pre-suppositions. The clinical work of analysts who think and work intersubjectively to a great extent involves the deconstruction of prereflective principles that have long organized a person's experience, or that have structured a particular intersubjective field, including the ideas, institutions, and practices of psycho-analysis itself (Rubin, in press). Our perspectival realism does not allow us the relativism implicit in more extreme postmodern views, but we find the questioning of categories, rigid dichotomies, and assumptions very congenial. In addition, the historical consciousness of thinkers like Derrida and Foucault—who consistently contextualize ideas and practices and study their genealogies—highlights the temporal and developmental perspective so necessary to psychoanalytic treatment.

The contextualisms of Wittgenstein and Bakhtin, and ours, should not be misunderstood as postmodernist relativism. The value of postmodernism's critical function is to remind us of our tendency to speak as if no historical origins or cultural-political meanings contextualized a particular idea or practice. Sometimes, however, *relativity* to particular contexts becomes con-fused with *relativism*, which treats frameworks as incommensu-rable and all interpretations as equally worthwhile because they come from different contexts (cf. Orange, 1995). Wittgenstein's view, Bakhtin's dialogism, and our perspectival realism allow us to evaluate and compare contexts themselves. One language-game may be more helpful, practical, or illuminating than another. Similarly, we may find certain psychoanalytic clinical theories, always embedded in frameworks of suppositions about human nature, more productive and intellectually coherent than others.

DYNAMIC, DYADIC, INTERSUBJECTIVE SYSTEMS

We have recently come upon a strain of thinking that helps to articulate the close connection between developmental thinking and our intersubjective contextualism.

A broad new scientific paradigm (Bertalanffy, 1968; Laszlo, 1972; Sucharov, 1994; Thelen and Smith, 1994) has been evolving from the investigation of phenomena that have variously been called dynamic, nonlinear, self-organizing, or chaotic systems. This new perspective is being employed in the search for common principles underlying the behavior of diverse physical, biological, and psychological phenomena. Dynamic systems theory is centrally concerned with the *process* of developmental change—that is, the generation of "emergent order and complexity: how structure and patterns arise from the cooperation of many individual parts" (Thelen and Smith, 1994, p. xiii). Because it accounts for the "messy, fluid, context-sensitive" (p. xvi) nature of developmental processes, we (Stolorow, in press) have contended that this framework is exceptionally well suited to serve as a source of guiding metaphors for psychoanalysis. We now suggest that it also provides a broad philosophical and scientific net in which all the variants of contextualism in psychoanalysis can find a home.[3]

Within a general systems philosophy, any living system is part of a hierarchy. Each system contains subsystems, or elements, that constitute the whole. Two or more systems interacting cooperatively form a suprasystem. From this perspective, the mental activity of the individual child or patient is a subsystem of the larger child-caregiver or patient-analyst suprasystem.[4] One- and two-person psychologies have tended to be reductive and incomplete because they proposed comprehensive explanatory theories grounded in one level only of a living systems hierarchy.

A dynamic systems account of a developmental process, whether occurring during childhood or in the psychoanalytic situation, rejects teleological conceptions of preordained end-states and preprogrammed epigenetic schemas. Instead, structure or pattern is seen to be *emergent* from "the self-organizing processes of continuously active living systems" (Thelen and Smith, 1994, p. 44). Emergent structure formation within a dynamic system develops from the intercoordination or cooperative interaction of its elements or subsystems as they coalesce into a self-organized pattern. From this perspective, for example, intractable repetitive

---

3. Thelen and Smith (1994) argue that dynamic systems theory "provides a biological rationale for contextualism" (p. xxi), a claim also exemplified in Edelman's (1992) "neural Darwinism."

4. Similarly, ideas form hierarchical systems. Ideas of greater generality (e.g., intersubjectivity or intrapsychic determinism) contextualize those that are more specific (e.g., particular clinical theories).

transferences and resistances seen clinically can be grasped as rigidly stable states of the patient-analyst system in which the analyst's stance has become tightly coordinated with the patient's grim expectations and fears of retraumatization.

Examples abound in the work of other relational theorists (Aron, 1996; Mitchell, 1988) and in our own of clinical phenomena viewed from a systems perspective. To list only a few, from Aron there is mutuality of analytic data generation and the coconstruction of meaning. In our work (Stolorow, Brandchaft, and Atwood, 1987; Stolorow and Atwood, 1992) there is a vision of psychopathological states, of multiple dimensions of transference, and of the boundary between conscious and unconscious, all as fluidly shifting properties of ongoing dynamic, dyadic, intersubjective systems.

TYPES OF CONTEXT CRUCIAL TO PSYCHOANALYTIC THINKING

Most prominent in current psychoanalytic thinking is the context of the analysand-analyst dyad. Relational theorists like Mitchell (1988), Hoffman (1983), Renik (1993), and Aron (1996) are providing not only extensive criticism of an exclusive theoretical and clinical focus on intrapsychic phenomena, but are also advocating continuous clinical attention to the analyst's contribution to clinical phenomena and to the formation and transformation of meanings. In our own work, we have insisted that analyst and patient form an indissoluble psychological system, and that neither can, without violence to the integrity of the analytic experience, be studied alone. The organizing activities of both participants in any psychoanalytic process are crucial to understanding the impasses and meanings that develop in a specific intersubjective field. When the process gets stuck, we do not think "the patient is resisting"; instead, we wonder how analyst and patient have coconstructed this logjam. We ask not only about the patient's history and organizing emotional convictions, but also about our own, as well as about what theoretical commitments might be trapping us in what Wittgenstein (1953) called "aspect-blindness." Aspect-blindness results from an inability to shift perspectives, to expand horizons, or to decenter (in the Piagetian sense—there is no implication that we can abandon our own subjectivity). So the first important contextual consideration—the here-and-now—includes the interacting subjective worlds and the organizing activities of both patient and analyst, including the analyst's theories and the cultural worlds of both participants.

Unfortunately, however, some relational theorists (Gill, 1982; Mitchell, 1988) restrict psychoanalytic inquiry primarily to the here-and-now, or snapshot context. They deride serious consideration of developmental contexts as infantilizing the patient, or as "developmental tilt." Probably their concern is a theoretical one that we share: developmental thinking can easily become reductionistic, or degenerate into mechanistic objectivism. If it does, we lose the complexity of psychological meanings, both found and formed in intersubjective systems, to a simplistic notion of causal genesis or etiology. We believe, however, that historical-developmental and cross-sectional contexts or dimensions cannot be so neatly distinguished and that we must accord serious attention to their interpenetration. Ontologically, we regard the past and the future as inevitably implicated in all present moments (Bergson, 1910). Epistemologically, we find it impossible to know an isolated moment. Clinically, we find ourselves, our patients, and our psychoanalytic work always embedded in constitutive *process*. Process means temporality and history. To work contextually is to work developmentally. To work developmentally is to maintain a continuing sensibility to past, present, and future experience. A good example of contextualist thinking in psychoanalysis is the work of Lichtenberg, Lachmann, and Fosshage (1992, 1996), who describe the ways in which context determines what developmentally shaped motivational system will be salient for a particular person at a particular time. Developmental thinking refuses the snapshot view—Derrida (1978) and Culler (1982) call this the "metaphysics of presence," or restriction to decontextualized moments or interactions (cf. Hayes, 1994)—and affirms the emotional life of persons who have come from somewhere and are going somewhere.

Unfortunately, serious attempts at relational thinking in psychoanalysis are still pervaded by atomist thinking. For example, Maroda's (1991) courageous and thoughtful book on countertransference claims that "the only tenable position for us to adopt is to focus on the nature of interaction and the emotional states of the therapist and the patient *at the moment* to determine what approach is most helpful within the realm of what is genuine and humanly possible" (p. 21). Without any developmental sensibility, a salutary emphasis on the personal presence and involvement of the analyst with the patient can slip into isolating the present moment. This "present-moment" thinking becomes the new rule of "technique" and leads to the overemphasis on countertransference disclosure. We have then two ahistorical, decontextualized Leibnizian windowless monads frozen into an isolated moment, trying to create windows. The irony is that extremely well-intentioned and thoughtful attempts to understand clinical process in relational ways are undermined by antirelational, antihistorical, decontextualized conceptions of human nature. Thinking contextually, on the contrary, means an ongoing sensitivity and relentless attention to context—developmental, relational, gender-related, cultural, and so on.

How does this work out in practice? Maureen, originally presenting at age 15 with anxiety that she related to her father's cancer and her sister's status as the family star, revealed after two years of treatment her obsessional terror that she might be lesbian. Endlessly she doubted her interest in boys, observable to all around her, and wondered if she was attracted to every girl who came within 50 feet of her. She suffered from rejection by one boyfriend after another—usually they were popular, extremely self-absorbed, and were seeing several girls at once. She worried that the problem was that she was not really straight. This pattern continued during her college years and worsened after her father's death in her freshman year. By her second year the thoughts so tortured her that she felt suicidal.

Many kinds of context demanded ongoing attention during the treatment of this patient. Her Irish Catholic family, composed of her mother, an older and a younger sister, and the dying father, had never spoken of sex, of sexuality, nor of emotion generally. There was no question in her family or in her cultural and religious surroundings that homosexuality could be anything but repulsive and sinful and sick. Any comment by her analyst about the common developmental questions of sexuality—implying that either gay or straight would be fine—sent her into a state of physically observable terror. A serious disjunction existed between the analyst's attitudes and the patient's panic. The analyst, who grew up in a similar cultural and religious world, still had difficulty understanding why the grip of this panic was so strong.

What seems to have helped eventually was the analyst's growing conviction that the worry about homosexuality concretized the patient's deeply held belief that she was evil, disgusting, and repulsive. This became clearer as she began to reveal her extensive and compulsive rituals from early and middle childhood, some of which persisted into early adulthood. All of these she had felt as necessary to ward off the punishment she so deeply believed she deserved for her "sins." Analyst and patient then began to study together the origins of the compulsions, the multiple contexts of their emergence, and the contexts (including treatment) in which they were being perpetuated. Analyzing the isolated experience of panic, even as it emerged in the treatment context, yielded little understanding and no relief. Investigating and illuminating the intersubjective origins and contexts of her shame and self-loathing, a topic which we will now consider in more general terms, were all-important to the reorganizing of her experience.

THINKING CONTEXTUALLY ABOUT SHAME AND SELF-LOATHING

It is our view that a consistent focus on the vicissitudes of self-experience leads inexorably to a recognition of the motivational primacy of affect, since affect, as the infant researchers have been amply demonstrating, is the prime organizer of self-experience within the developmental system. A shift from drive to affectivity as the central motivational construct for psychoanalysis represents a shift from an intrapsychic to an intersubjective paradigm. From birth onward, affective experience is regulated, or misregulated, within intersubjective systems of reciprocal mutual influence (Beebe, Jaffe, and Lachmann, 1992). As one of us (Stolorow, Brandchaft, and Atwood, 1987), in a chapter written in collaboration with Daphne Stolorow, stated it,

> Affects can be seen as organizers of self-experience throughout development, if met with the requisite affirming, accepting, differentiating, synthesizing, and containing responses from caregivers. An absence of steady, attuned responsiveness to the child's affect states leads to ... significant

derailments of optimal affect integration and to a propensity
to dissociate or disavow affective reactions [p. 67].

It is in such derailments of the process of affect integration, we
contend, that the intersubjective roots of shame can be found.

A basic idea of intersubjectivity theory is that recurring patterns of intersubjective transaction within the developmental
system result in the establishment of invariant principles that
unconsciously organize the child's subsequent experiences
(Stolorow and Atwood, 1992). It is these unconscious ordering
principles, forged within the crucible of the child-caregiver system, that form the basic building blocks of personality development. Increasingly, we have found that those principles that
unconsciously organize the experience of affect are of greatest
import clinically. From early, recurring experiences of malattunement, the child acquires the unconscious conviction that
unmet developmental yearnings and reactive feeling states are
manifestations of a loathsome defect or of an inherent inner
badness. A defensive self-ideal is established, representing a
self-image purified of the offending affect states that were perceived to be intolerable to the early surround. Living up to this
affectively purified ideal becomes a central requirement for
maintaining harmonious ties to caregivers and for upholding
self-esteem. Thereafter, the emergence of prohibited affect is
experienced as a failure to embody the required ideal, an expo-
sure of the underlying essential defectiveness or badness, and
is accompanied by feelings of isolation, shame, and self-
loathing.

Broucek (1991) has offered an account of the intersubjective
origins of shame that emphasizes the caregiver's failure to
respond supportively to the child's experiences of efficacy and
intentionality, resulting in the child's acquiring a painful sense of
being viewed as an object rather than as a subject. In our language, Broucek understands shame to originate in malattunement to affect states that have in common elements of
excitement, pride, and pleasure in one's own functioning. We, in
contrast, believe that shame can derive from malattunement to
any significant aspect of the child's affectivity, including both the
joyful affective experiences that accompany developmental
progress and the painful reactive affect states evoked by injuries
and disruptions.

To illustrate the theoretical and clinical advantages of conceptualizing both narcissistic disturbance and shame in terms of the
fate of affect within an intersubjective system, we turn to a recon-
sideration of the dissociative processes that Kohut (1971) believed
were pathognomonic in certain narcissistic personality disorders.
Kohut theorized that when the child's archaic grandiosity
encounters massive, traumatic deflations, then the grandiosity
and the child's longings for the caregiver's mirroring participa-
tion in it undergo repression in order to prevent retraumatization. The consequences of this experiential sequestering of archaic
grandiosity beneath a repression barrier—what Kohut called a
"horizontal split in the psyche"—are symptoms of narcissistic
depletion, such as feelings of emptiness, deadness, and worthlessness. In the most common type of narcissistic personality,
Kohut believed, the depletion symptoms alternate in experience
with states of conscious, noisy, imperious grandiosity. The noisily
grandiose and depleted states are separated from one another by
a "vertical split"—by disavowal rather than repression.

As useful as Kohut's formulation may have been, it was seriously marred by his use of the same term, "grandiose self," to
refer both to what was traumatically deflated and repressed and
to what is being imperiously expressed. In so doing, Kohut con-
flated two organizations of experience that have distinctly different origins and meanings. We believe that what was deflated
and sequestered under a horizontal split is best termed *archaic
expansiveness*, a phrase referring to the broad range of joyful
affective experiences that accompany developmental progress.
The imperiousness, arrogance, entitlement, and contempt segregated on one side of the vertical split, by contrast, are best captured by the term *defensive grandiosity*. It is defensive in at least
three senses.

First, to the extent that this grandiosity arises out of an identification with the defensive self-ideal discussed earlier, it represents an accommodation to a caregiver's narcissistic use of the
child's qualities and performance. As Bacal and Newman (1990)
have pointed out, this attempt to maintain a bond through compliance with the caregiver's emotional requirements is analogous to Winnicott's (1960) concept of the "false self" (see also
Brandchaft, 1993).

Second, insofar as the defensive grandiosity contains elements
of "splendid isolation," omnipotent self-sufficiency, and

devaluation of others, it buttresses the repression of the horizontally split-off developmental longings for connection—in this instance, longings for mirroring affirmation of the deflated archaic expansiveness.

It must be remembered that caregivers who repeatedly deflate a child's expansiveness are unlikely to respond with attunement and understanding to the child's painful emotional reactions to these deflations. The child, therefore, is likely to perceive that his or her painful reactive affect states are unwelcome or damaging to the caregivers and therefore must be sacrificed in order to maintain the needed ties. Thus the third, and perhaps most important, defensive function of the noisy grandiosity is that it serves to disavow the affective pain on the other side of the vertical split, feelings that were perceived to be unacceptable to the surround, manifestations of a loathsome defect that had to be eliminated.

Intense shame reactions can be evoked along either of these two splits. The breakthrough of archaic expansiveness into conscious experience is usually accompanied by anticipatory shame, not, as Kohut (1972) claimed, because of a "psychoeconomic imbalance," but because the person expects to encounter the same traumatic deflations that the expansiveness originally received from caregivers. Challenges to, or puncturings of, the defensive grandiosity generally also produce shame, because they threaten to expose the disavowed vulnerability and pain that have come to be organized as irrefutable evidence of an underlying immutable flaw. It is here that narcissistic rage and destructiveness are readily called into play, in a desperate attempt to restore the defensive grandiosity and rid one's self-experience of the unbearable shame (Kohut, 1972; Stolorow, 1984; Morrison, 1989).

The most deleterious clinical consequence of Kohut's failure to distinguish conceptually between archaic expansiveness and defensive grandiosity is that it has led to the mistaken belief that it is therapeutically beneficial to "mirror" defensive grandiosity, which is tantamount to colluding with the defense and can foster addiction to the analyst's "responsiveness." In our experience, the most effective approach to defensive grandiosity is neither to mirror nor to puncture it, but to wait for openings in it—that is, for opportunities to make contact with the painful affect walled off on the other side of the vertical split. Such efforts invariably evoke intense shame in the transference, as the patient feels convinced that the analyst can only react with secret revulsion and contempt to the defectiveness that has been exposed. The investigation, interpretation, and working through of this shame, and of the organizing principles from which it derives, are crucial in the establishment of a therapeutic bond in which the disavowed affective pain can be integrated and the defensive grandiosity can become less necessary. With the establishment of an expectation that painful emotional reactions to injuries and disruptions can evoke acceptance and understanding rather than disdain, an expanding zone of safety is created wherein the patient can dare to bring primary developmental longings into the open and expose them to the analyst.

It was this process of understanding within a slowly expanding zone of safety that made it possible for Maureen to develop a reorganized, less shame-ridden self-experience. As she found relief from her obsessional and compulsive symptoms, including her sense of a fatal flaw within her own sexuality, she became able to live a satisfying life without the shame and self-loathing.

Let us now turn to a more detailed discussion of dissociation processes and their intersubjective origins.

THINKING CONTEXTUALLY ABOUT DISSOCIATION AND MULTIPLICITY

After Freud rethought the seduction theory he had formed in the 1890s, dissociation was relegated to the periphery of the psychoanalytic purview. Our purpose here, in the context of contemporary awareness of childhood trauma, is to examine the concept of dissociation once again, this time from an intersubjective viewpoint. We temporarily bypass the problem of defining *dissociation*, because each historical figure who considered it used this term in his own distinctive way. Clinical experience leads us to expect that we need a contextualist concept of dissociation to do psychoanalytic work that recognizes the intersubjective genesis and maintenance of much pathology.

Freud became interested in dissociation during his studies with Charcot (Ellenberger, 1970), for whom dissociation was an essential marker of hysteria, and for whom, conversely, hysteria was an accurate diagnosis for those who dissociate. We can see

the influence of Charcot in Breuer and Freud's (1893–1895)
Studies in Hysteria.

> The splitting of consciousness which is so striking in the
> well-known classical cases under the form of "double con-
> science" is present to a rudimentary degree in every hysteria
> and . . . a tendency to such a dissociation, and with it the
> emergence of abnormal states of consciousness (which we
> shall bring together under the term 'hypnoid'), is the basic
> phenomenon of this neurosis. . . . these hypnoid states share
> with one another and with hypnosis. . . . one common fea-
> ture: the ideas which emerge in them are very intense but
> are cut off from associate communication with the rest of the
> content of consciousness [p. 12].

This formulation suffers, as Fairbairn pointed out in his early
thesis (1929), from the atomism inherent in associationist psychology. In Fairbairn's words, "the mind does not consist in an
aggregation of separate elements or functions, one of which can
be split off from the rest without any effect except its loss"
(p. 33). Unlike his contemporary and rival Pierre Janet, who
continued to hold this view of dissociation, Freud later developed a somewhat more holistic view of the mind.
Unfortunately, Freud also abandoned any interest in dissociation as a distinct process, turning instead to repression, conceived as active and motivated.
He returned to dissociation only briefly and indirectly. In "The
Ego and the Id" (1923), Freud speculated that it consisted in the
residues of object relations.

> If [ego identifications] obtain the upper hand and become too
> numerous, unduly powerful and incompatible with one
> another, a pathological outcome will not be far off. It may
> come to a disruption of the ego in consequence of the differ-
> ent identifications becoming cut off from one another by
> resistances, perhaps the secret of the case of what is
> described as "multiple personality" is that the different iden-
> tifications seize hold of consciousness in turn [pp. 30–31].

Perhaps sensing the inadequacy of this formulation, Freud
remained committed to repression as the fundamental mecha-

nism of unconsciousness. Memory loss was an active and motivated process of forgetting, required for maintaining intrapsychic equilibrium.

Fairbairn was dissatisfied with the choice of repression over dissociation that seemed to be required of Freudians. Noting that in what was then the conventional view of dissociation, "elements of mental life, which are ordinarily conscious, become split off from the main body of consciousness and maintain a high degree of independence," he held with Janet (1907) that the independence in question concerned activity rather than consciousness. Aspects of personality, whether or not characterized by independent consciousness, function in ways that seem cut off from the rest of personality. Fairbairn concluded that dissociation was quite a normal process, or at least "not necessarily abnormal" (p. 35). "A perfectly normal accompaniment of emotion" (p. 37), dissociation became for Fairbairn,

> an active mental process, whereby unacceptable mental content or an unacceptable mental function becomes cut off from personal consciousness, without thereby ceasing to be mental—such mental content or mental function being regarded as unacceptable if it is either irrelevant to, incompatible with or unpleasant in relation to an active interest [p. 78].

Fairbairn considered four possibilities for the relationship of dissociation and repression: (1) that dissociation was a form of repression, or suppression, as Rivers (1924) had claimed; (2) that dissociation and repression are entirely distinct, as McDougall (1926), under the influence of Jung's personality types, had claimed; (3) that the two processes are identical, dismissed immediately by Fairbairn because sleep, fatigue, hypnotic and drug-induced states cannot be understood as repression; and (4) that dissociation is the larger category, and that repression is a special form of dissociation. His arguments against the first two possibilities, and for the last, are carefully articulated but too long to summarize here.

The consequences, however, of adopting the last choice are important, both for the turn Fairbairn's own thinking later took, and for the intersubjective conception we are articulating. Here is Fairbairn's formulation of the distinction between repression and dissociation, and of their precise relationship.

Its nature [the nature of repression] is best understood in the
light of the term, which Freud originally employed when he
first isolated the process—viz., that of "defence" [Fairbairn's
spelling]. Defence, however is a feature which repression
shares with all forms of dissociation of the unpleasant. The
difference between repression and simple dissociation of
the unpleasant lies in the fact, that in the first case the men-
ace, from which protection is sought, is of *internal* origin,
whereas in the second case it is only of *external* origin. In
simple dissociation of the unpleasant, the defence is
directed against mental content determined ultimately by
events that happen to the individual. In repression, the
defence is directed against *tendencies which form part of the
mental structure* of the individual himself [p. 77].

Let us look carefully at this formulation, remembering that it
long predates Fairbairn's later radical rethinking of the most
basic assumptions of psychoanalytic theory. First of all, repression and what Fairbairn calls "simple dissociation" are grouped
together under the more general category of "forms of dissociation of the unpleasant." Second, the most obvious quality of
repression proper here is its intrapsychic, or isolated-mind,
nature. People are thought to have unacceptable internal sexual
and aggressive tendencies, and actively, if not deliberately, make
these disappear quite permanently from consciousness.
Repression thus amounts to active dissociation of unpleasant or
intolerable or conflict-arousing tendencies within the person.
This formulation makes it clear that the classical conception of
repression is inextricably bound up with drive theory, and with
the isolated-mind assumption (Stolorow and Atwood, 1992).
    This view of repression, as well as Fairbairn's whole formula-
tion of the distinction between repression and dissociation, further depends on a problematic bifurcation of interiority and
exteriority. Once we accept the intersubjectivity principle, we
cannot distinguish so neatly between *events that happen* and *tendencies which form part of the mental structure*. We must insist, on
the contrary, that there is no mental structure without intersubjective context, and that there are no "events that happen" without a person to perceive them and construe their meaning. *In any
psychologically significant sense*, if the tree falls in the forest and no
one perceives it, nothing happened. What "happens" is what

happens to and for a person. Even more important, what happens is what happens to and for someone in an intersubjective context.

Wittgenstein's notion of "seeing as," closely related to the foregrounds and backgrounds of Gestalt psychology, describes better the meaning of dissociation. Because of the context—for our purposes, intersubjective context—of whatever we experience, we see it as a certain thing, a duck or a rabbit, for example. To organize our experience into a "seeing as" we must, of course, take a perspective that hides much from view. We can call this hiding *dissociation* and recognize that much of it goes on automatically, according to previously organized emotional convictions or organizing principles, prereflectively unconscious (Stolorow and Atwood, 1992). This contextualist view removes the atomism involved in Fairbairn's conception of dissociation and obviates the need for the Freudian conception of repression. We now can see dissociation as temporary or more permanent hiding of aspects of experience according to patterns of organizing activity, intersubjectively formed and maintained.

What, we may ask, then happens to Kohut's (1971) distinction between the vertical and horizontal split in personality? Vertical splitting resembled dissociation, and horizontal splitting was like Freudian repression. Does not horizontal splitting or repression create the dynamic unconscious previously described? Dynamically unconscious experiences, if articulated or expressed, would threaten vital ties (Stolorow and Atwood, 1992). Only if we reformulate repression as an intersubjective process can we save it from Cartesian isolation and render it adequately contextual. Further, we must recognize the stretching involved in reformulating an idea with such close ties to drive-theoretical, atomistic, and objectivist points of view. Horizontal splitting, corresponding to repression, from our viewpoint involves a relatively permanent or enduring "seeing-as" that excludes certain potential contents of awareness from becoming conscious. Vertical splitting, on the other hand, refers to the experiential segregation of differing perspectives, and thus alternating "seeings-as," each of which has its own distinctive organization of foreground and background, its pattern of disclosure and hiddenness.

We think of dissociation as a Janus-faced phenomenon. On one side it reflects the separating of oneself from events and circumstances that produce such disruptive and disintegrative affect states that they cannot become a part of any ongoing self-structure or conscious sense of identity and history. On the other side it reflects an emotional environment that did not provide the validation and acknowledgment necessary to render those events assimilable (Stolorow and Atwood, 1992). Dissociation shields the child from disruptive pain, but it also represents a form of pathological accommodation to an environment in which there is no space for that pain to exist (Brandchaft, 1994).

Let us briefly return to the related discussion of multiple and unitary selves in recent psychoanalytic literature. Mitchell (1993), Bromberg (1996), and others suggest that the integrated or unitary self is an illusion and argue for the priority of spatial over temporal (continuity-oriented) metaphors in speaking of self-experience. Lachmann (1996), on the other hand, believes that an adequately process-oriented understanding of personal strivings for integration does justice to the multiplicity as well as to the wholeness of human experience. Our contextualist, systems point of view transcends this debate, which tends to confuse the organization of experience (inevitable) with the experience of organization (not inevitable). We see disorganization (read *dissociation, multiplicity*) as part of a dynamic system's self-organizing process. There is no disrespect for the one or for the many, for cohesion or for dissociation, here. Nor do we mean to imply that they simply coexist in some irreducible paradox or dialectical tension, as some relational theorists would claim (Ghent, 1992; Hoffman, 1994; Aron, 1996). The one and the many are alternative organizations of subjectivity, shifting in experiential prominence within specific intersubjective contexts.

CONCLUSION: CONTEXTUALIST SENSIBILITIES AND ATTITUDES

We have earlier said that our intersubjective perspective is not a clinical theory, but a metatheory, or a set of questions for theories. Even more, from a clinical standpoint, we are describing a sensibility that informs our thinking and our work. We can describe this sensibility, in part and in a fallibilistic spirit, in terms of attitudes. The essence of psychoanalytic work does not lie in any specific concrete procedure that must be employed, but rather is constituted by an *attitude* the clinician brings to the material and by a *process* that takes place in the ensuing dialogue with the patient. The attitude is one of empathic-introspective inquiry, which gives rise to a therapeutic interaction that illuminates (and eventually transforms) the meanings and patterns that organize the patient's experience. The process cannot possibly be determined or defined by concrete situational factors (e.g., the face-to-face encounter, the use of the couch, the frequency or length of sessions, and the like). True, in any given case, specific concrete arrangements may facilitate or hinder the analytic work, but to conceive narrowly of the psychoanalytic process as depending on any specific set of such arrangements is to fall into the illusion of seeing psychoanalysis as actually analogous to a medical procedure or a technique of production, as we noted earlier. To the extent that the analyst is restricted in how he or she conducts the treatment, in terms of rules of abstinence or any other "rules" one might formulate (even the rule of "free" association), psychoanalytic practice begins to resemble the frozen rituals that are closely associated with dogmatic religious faith. Like Lindon (1994, in press), we point to the possibility of an emancipation of analysts in both their thinking and their practice, a freeing that would enable them to use the full resources of their creativity in the tasks of psychoanalytic exploration and treatment.

A contextualist view leads inevitably to a self-reflexive attitude that remains perpetually open to new dimensions of action and experience. Unlike certain postmodern nihilisms, fallibilism (Orange, 1995) characterizes both the thought and the practice of a contextualist. From an epistemological point of view, we recognize that our present understanding of anything or anyone is only a perspective within a horizon inevitably limited by the historicity of our own organized and organizing experience. From the viewpoint of practice, a contextualist holds lightly not only theory, but any particular view of meaning in the patient's experience, or in the cocreated experience in the intersubjective field of treatment. This fallibilistic attitude keeps us flexible and open to multiple and emerging contexts of meaning. Contexualism does not prescribe "technique" (see chapter two), not even the technique of considering many clinical questions at once; rather it creates an attitude that opens our horizons to expanded possibilities of meaning and ensures that our theoretical ideas continue to evolve toward an ever-widening and more encompassing viewpoint. Contextualist thinking in itself is neither theory nor practice, but it includes attitudes or sensibilities in relation to both theory and practice.

Contextualist attitudes and sensibilities, with their fallibilistic bent, lend themselves well to the creative and playful spirit that Winnicott (1971) advocated in psychoanalytic practice (Rubin, in press). If we can identify the contexts that have led to a particular experiential organization, we can play with it, question it, and experiment with its reorganization.

Epilogue

The process by which intersubjectivity theory has developed over the past two decades mirrors and expresses the central concept around which this point of view has come into being. The idea of the intersubjective field, understood as a system of interacting, differently organized subjective worlds, emerged from the intersection of the various personal and intellectual perspectives each of the participants brought to the ongoing collaboration. We have repeatedly found it possible, through the bringing together of our differing and complementary backgrounds, to develop ideas that would not have been possible for any of us working and thinking alone.

In the spirit of the self-reflections offered in the concluding section of *Faces in a Cloud* (1993), we now want to take up what intersubjectivity theory has meant to the present authors. Each of us has brought his or her own specific emotional needs into this working together and has found an experience of what we have sought, both in the ideas generated and in the collaboration itself. Our emotional histories have included shattering early experiences of loss, of invalidation and usurpation, and of crushing devaluation. Our work together in developing a contextualist understanding of intersubjectivity theory has provided for each of us a pathway toward restoration and hope. It has meant the finding of enduring personal friendships, the discovery of deep and reliable validation, and the experience of being found as a valued collaborator in a shared enterprise of emotional understanding. For each of us, intersubjective contextualism overcomes isolation and affirms a sense of personal meaning in belonging and contributing to the human world.

References

Aristotle (322 BCE). *Nicomachean Ethics*, trans. T. Irwin. Indianapolis: Hackett, 1985.

Aron, L. (1996). *A Meeting of Minds: Mutuality in Psychoanalysis.* Hillsdale, NJ: The Analytic Press.

Atwood, G. & Stolorow, R. (1980). Psychoanalytic concepts and the representational world. *Psychoanalysis and Contemporary Thought,* 3:267–290.

———— & ———— (1984). *Structures of Subjectivity: Explorations in Psychoanalytic Phenomenology.* Hillsdale, NJ: The Analytic Press.

———— & ———— (1993). *Faces in a Cloud: Intersubjectivity in Personality Theory,* 2nd ed. Northvale, NJ: Aronson.

———— & Tomkins, S. (1976). On the subjectivity of personality theory. *Journal of the History of the Behavioral Sciences,* 12:166–177.

Bacal, H. & Newman, K. (1990). *Theories of Object Relations: Bridges to Self Psychology.* New York: Columbia University Press.

Bakhtin, M. (1981). *The Dialogic Imagination.* Austin: University of Texas Press.

Barratt, B. (1993). *Psychoanalysis and the Postmodern Impulse: Knowing and Being Since Freud's Psychology.* Baltimore: Johns Hopkins University Press.

Barrett, W. (1979). *The Illusion of Technique.* Garden City, NY: Doubleday.

Beebe, B., Jaffe, J. & Lachmann, F. (1992). A dyadic systems view of communication. In: *Relational Perspectives in Psychoanalysis,* ed. N. Skolnick & S. Warshaw. Hillsdale, NJ: The Analytic Press, pp. 61–81.

Bergmann, M. & Hartman, F. (1976). *The Evolution of Psychoanalytic Technique.* New York: Columbia University Press.

Bergson, H. (1910). *Time and Free Will,* trans. F. Pogson. New York: Harper Torchbooks, 1960.

Bernstein, R. (1983). *Beyond Objectivism and Relativism: Science, Hermeneutics, and Praxis.* Philadelphia: University of Pennsylvania Press.

Bertalanffy, L. (1968). *General Systems Theory.* New York: Braziller.

Bleuler, E. (1911). *Dementia Praecox or the Group of Schizophrenias.* Madison, CT: International Universities Press, 1987.

Bollas, C. (1987). *The Shadow of the Object: Psychoanalysis of the Unthought Known.* London: Free Association Books.

Bouveresse, J. (1995). *Wittgenstein Reads Freud: The Myth of the Unconscious,* trans. C. Cosman. Princeton, NJ: Princeton University Press.

Brandchaft, B. (1993). To free the spirit from its cell. In: *The Intersubjective Perspective*, ed. R. Stolorow, G. Atwood & B. Brandchaft. Northvale, NJ: Aronson, 1994, pp. 57–76.

——— (1994). *Structures of pathological accommodation and change in analysis*. Presented at the Association for Psychoanalytic Self Psychology, New York City.

Breuer, J. & Freud, S. (1893–1895). Studies on hysteria. *Standard Edition*, 2. London: Hogarth Press, 1951.

Bromberg, P. (1996). Standing in the spaces: The multiplicity of self and the psychoanalytic relationship. *Contemporary Psychoanalysis*, 32:509–536.

Broucek, F. (1991). *Shame and the Self*. New York: Guilford.

Carver, N. (1994). *This Complicated Form of Life: Essays on Wittgenstein*. Chicago: Open Court.

Culler, J. (1982). *On Deconstruction*. Ithaca, NY: Cornell University Press.

Derrida, J. (1978). *Writing and Difference*, trans. A. Bass. Chicago: University of Chicago Press.

Edelman, G. (1992). *Bright Air, Brilliant Fire*. New York: Basic Books.

Ehrenberg, D. (1992). *The Intimate Edge: Extending the Reach of Psychoanalytic Interaction*. New York: Norton.

Eissler, K. R. (1958). Remarks on some variations in psychoanalytical technique. *International Journal of Psycho-Analysis*, 39:222–229.

Ellenberger, H. (1970). *The Discovery of the Unconscious*. London: Penguin Books.

Etchegoyen, R. (1991). *The Fundamentals of Psychoanalytic Technique*. London: Karnac.

Fairbairn, R. (1929). Dissociation and repression. In: *From Instinct to Self: Selected Papers of W.R.D. Fairbairn, Vol. II*, ed. E. Birtles & D. Scharff. Northvale, NJ: Aronson, 1994, pp. 13–79.

Federn, P. (1926). Some variations in ego feeling. *International Journal of Psycho-Analysis*, 7:434–444.

Flax, J. (1996). Taking multiplicity seriously: Some consequences for psychoanalytic theorizing and practice. *Contemporary Psychoanalysis*, 32:577–594.

Fourcher, L. (1996). The authority of logic and the logic of authority: The import of the Grunbaum debate for psychoanalytically informed psychotherapy. *Psychoanalytic Dialogues*, 6:515–532.

Freud, A. (1936). *The Ego and the Mechanisms of Defense*. New York: International Universities Press, 1946.

Freud, S. (1900). The interpretation of dreams. *Standard Edition*, 5:509–622. London: Hogarth Press, 1953.

——— (1911). Psychoanalytic notes on an autobiographical account of paranoia. *Standard Edition*, 12:9–79. London: Hogarth Press, 1957.

———— (1912). Recommendations to physicians practising psycho-analysis. *Standard Edition*, 12:109–120. London: Hogarth Press, 1958.

———— (1913). The claims of psycho-analysis to scientific interest. *Standard Edition*, 13:165–190. London: Hogarth Press, 1958.

———— (1915). Observations on transference love. *Standard Edition*, 12:158–171. London: Hogarth Press, 1958.

———— (1919). Lines of advance in psycho-analytic therapy. *Standard Edition*, 17:157–168. London: Hogarth Press, 1955.

———— (1923). The ego and the id. *Standard Edition*, 19:3–59. London: Hogarth Press, 1962.

———— (1933 [1932]). New introductory lectures on psycho-analysis. *Standard Edition*, 22:5–182. London: Hogarth Press, 1964.

Gadamer, H. (1975a). Hermeneutics and social science. *Cultural Hermeneutics*, 2:307–16.

———— (1975b). *Truth and Method*, trans. J. Weisheimer & D. Marshall, 2nd ed. New York: Crossroads, 1991.

———— (1979). The problem of historical consciousness. In: *Interpretive Social Science: A Reader*, ed. P. Rabinow & W. Sullivan. Berkeley: University of California Press, pp. 103–160.

Ghent, E. (1992). Paradox and process. *Psychoanalytic Dialogues*, 2:135–159.

Gill, M. (1982). *Analysis of Transference, Vol. 1*. New York: International Universities Press.

———— (1984). Psychoanalysis and psychotherapy: A revision. *International Review of Psycho-Analysis*, 11:161–180.

Greenson, R. (1967). *The Technique and Practice of Psychoanalysis, Vol. 1*. New York: International Universities Press.

Grunbaum, A. (1984). *The Foundations of Psychoanalysis: A Philosophical Critique*. Berkeley: University of California Press.

Guntrip, H. (1969). *Schizoid Phenomena, Object Relations and the Self*. New York: International Universities Press.

Harris, A. (1996). The conceptual power of multiplicity. *Contemporary Psychoanalysis*, 32:537–552.

Hayes, G. (1994). Empathy: A conceptual and clinical deconstruction. *Psychoanalytic Dialogues*, 4:409–424.

Hegel, G. (1907). *The Phenomenology of Spirit*, trans. A. Miller. Oxford: Oxford University Press, 1977.

Hoffman, I. (1983). The patient as interpreter of the analyst's experience. *Contemporary Psychoanalysis*, 19:389–422.

———— (1991). Discussion: Toward a social-constructivist view of the psychoanalytic situation. *Psychoanalytic Dialogues*, 1:74–105.

———— (1994). Dialectical thinking and therapeutic action in the psychoanalytic process. *Psychoanalytic Quarterly*, 63:187–218.

Janet, P. (1907). *The Major Symptoms of Hysteria*. London: Macmillan.

Jones, J. (1995). *Affects as Process*. Hillsdale, NJ: The Analytic Press.

Kerr, M. & Bowen, M. (1988). *Family Evaluation*. New York: Norton.

Kohut, H. (1959). Introspection, empathy, and psychoanalysis: An examination of the relationship between mode of observation and theory. In: *The Search for the Self, Vol. 1*, ed. P. Ornstein. Madison, CT: International Universities Press, pp. 205–232.

———— (1971). *The Analysis of the Self*. New York: International Universities Press.

———— (1972). Thoughts on narcissism and narcissistic rage. *The Psychoanalytic Study of the Child*, 27:360–400. New Haven, CT: Yale University Press.

———— (1977). *The Restoration of the Self*. Madison, CT: International Universities Press.

———— (1980). Reflections on Advances in Self Psychology. In: *Advances in Self Psychology*, ed. A. Goldberg. Madison, CT: International Universities Press, pp. 473–554.

Kundera, M. (1984). *The Unbearable Lightness of Being*. New York: Harper & Row.

Lachmann, F. (1996). How many selves make a person? *Contemporary Psychoanalysis*, 32:595–614.

Langs, R. (1978). *Technique in Transition*. New York: Aronson.

Laszlo, E. (1972). *Introduction to Systems Philosophy*. New York: Gordon and Breach.

Lichtenberg, J. D. (1983). The influence of values and value judgments on the psychoanalytic encounter. *Psychoanalytic Inquiry*, 3:647–664.

———— Lachmann, F. & Fosshage, J. (1992). *Self and Motivational Systems: Toward a Theory of Psychoanalytic Technique*. Hillsdale, NJ: The Analytic Press.

———— ———— & ———— (1996). *The Clinical Exchange: Techniques Derived from Self and Motivational Systems*. Hillsdale, NJ: The Analytic Press.

Lindon, J. (1994). Gratification and provision in psychoanalysis: Should we get rid of "the rule of abstinence"? *Psychoanalytic Dialogues*, 4:549–582.

———— (in press). A case report of the treatment of a brutally traumatized man.

Mannheim, K. (1936). *Ideology and Utopia*. New York: Harcourt Brace and World.

Maroda, K. (1991). *The Power of Countertransference*. Northvale, NJ: Aronson.

McDougall, W. (1926). *Outline of Abnormal Psychology*. London: Methuen.

Mitchell, S. (1988). *Relational Concepts in Psychoanalysis: An Integration*. Cambridge, MA: Harvard University Press.

———— (1993). *Hope and Dread in Psychoanalysis*. New York: Basic Books.

Monk, R. (1990). *Ludwig Wittgenstein: The Duty of Genius*. New York: Penguin Books.

Morrison, A. (1989). *Shame: The Underside of Narcissism*. Hillsdale, NJ: The Analytic Press.

—— & Stolorow, R. (1997). Shame, narcissism, and intersubjectivity. In: *New Perspectives on Shame*, ed. M. Lansky & A. Morrison. Hillsdale, NJ: The Analytic Press.

Murray, H. (1938). *Explorations in Personality*. New York: Science Editions.

Niederland, W. (1984). *The Schreber Case*, 2nd ed. Hillsdale, NJ: The Analytic Press.

Nunberg, H. (1951). Transference and reality. *International Journal of Psycho-Analysis*, 32:1–9.

Orange, D. (1994). Countertransference, empathy, and the hermeneutical circle. In: *The Intersubjective Perspective*, ed. R. Stolorow, G. Atwood & B. Brandchaft. Northvale, NJ: Aronson, pp. 177–186.

—— (1995). *Emotional Understanding: Studies in Psychoanalytic Epistemology*. New York: Guilford.

Panel (1987). Conversion of psychotherapy to psychoanalysis, C.P. Fisher, reporter. *Journal of the American Psychoanalytic Association*, 35:713–726.

Polanyi, M. (1958). *Personal Knowledge*. Chicago: University of Chicago Press.

Putnam, H. (1990). *Realism with a Human Face*. Cambridge, MA: Harvard University Press.

Raphling, D. (1995). Interpretation and expectations. *Journal of the American Psychoanalytic Association*, 43:95–111.

Renik, O. (1993). Analytic interaction: Conceptualizing technique in light of the analyst's irreducible subjectivity. *Psychoanalytic Quarterly*, 62:553–571.

—— (1995). The ideal of the anonymous analyst and the problem of self-disclosure. *Psychoanalytic Quarterly*, 64:466–495.

—— (1996). The perils of neutrality. *Psychoanalytic Quarterly*, 65:495–517.

Rivers, W. (1924). *Instinct and the Unconscious*. Cambridge: Cambridge University Press.

Rubin, J. (in press). *A Psychoanalysis for Our Time*. New York: New York University Press.

Schatzman, M. (1973). *Soul Murder: Persecution in the Family*. New York: Random House.

Singer, E. (1977). The fiction of analytic anonymity. In: *The Human Dimension in Psychoanalysis*, ed. K. Frank. New York: Grune & Stratton.

Spence, D. (1993). The hermeneutic turn: Soft science or loyal opposition? *Psychoanalytic Dialogues*, 3:1–10.

Stern, D. N. (1985). *The Interpersonal World of the Infant*. New York: Basic Books.

Stolorow, R. (1978). The concept of psychic structure: Its metapsychological and clinical psychoanalytic meanings. *International Review of Psycho-Analysis*, 5:313–320.

———— (1984). Aggression in the psychoanalytic situation. In: *The Intersubjective Perspective*, ed. R. Stolorow, G. Atwood & B. Brandchaft. Northvale, NJ: Aronson, 1994, pp. 113–119.

———— (1995). Introduction: Tensions between loyalism and expansionism in self psychology. In: *Progress in Self Psychology, Volume 11, The Impact of New Ideas*, ed. A. Goldberg. Hillsdale, NJ: The Analytic Press, pp. xi–xvii.

———— (in press). Principles of dynamic systems, intersubjectivity, and the obsolete distinction between one-person and two-person psychologies: Commentary on Lewis Aron's *A Meeting of Minds*. *Psychoanalytic Dialogues*.

———— & Atwood, G. (1979). *Faces in a Cloud: Subjectivity in Personality Theory*. New York: Aronson.

———— & ———— (1992). *Contexts of Being: The Intersubjective Foundations of Psychological Life*. Hillsdale, NJ: The Analytic Press.

———— & Lachmann, F. (1980). *Psychoanalysis of Developmental Arrests*. Madison, CT: International Universities Press.

———— & ———— (1984/1985). Transference: The future of an illusion. *The Annual of Psychoanalysis*, 12/13:19–38. Madison, CT: International Universities Press.

———— Atwood, G. & Brandchaft, B., eds. (1994). *The Intersubjective Perspective*. Northvale, NJ: Aronson.

———— Brandchaft, B. & Atwood, G. (1987). *Psychoanalytic Treatment: An Intersubjective Approach*. Hillsdale, NJ: The Analytic Press.

Stone, L. (1961). *The Psychoanalytic Situation*. New York: International Universities Press.

Sucharov, M. (1994). Psychoanalysis, self psychology, and intersubjectivity. In: *The Intersubjective Perspective*, ed. R. Stolorow, G. Atwood & B. Brandchaft. Northvale, NJ: Aronson, pp. 187–202.

Tausk, V. (1917). On the origin of the influencing machine in schizophrenia. *Psychoanalytic Quarterly*, 2:519–556.

Taylor, C. (1985). Atomism. In: *Philosophy and the Human Sciences, Vol. 2*. Cambridge: Cambridge University Press.

———— (1989). *Sources of the Self: The Making of the Modern Identity*. Cambridge, MA: Harvard University Press.

Thelen, E. & Smith, L.(1994). *A Dynamic Systems Approach to the Development of Cognition and Action*. Cambridge, MA: MIT Press.

Thomson, P. (1991). Countertransference. In: *The Intersubjective Perspective*, ed. R. Stolorow, G. Atwood & B. Brandchaft. Northvale, NJ: Aronson, 1994, pp. 127–143.

Tomkins, S. (1963). *Affect, Imagery, Consciousness, Vol. 2: The Negative Affects.* New York: Springer.

—— (1991). *Affect, Imagery, Consciousness, Vol. 3: Anger and Fear.* New York: Springer.

Wachtel, P. (1993). *Therapeutic Communication: Principles and Effective Practice.* New York: Guilford.

Winnicott, D. (1958). *Through Paediatrics to Psycho-Analysis.* New York: Basic Books.

—— (1960). Ego distortion in terms of true and false self. In: *The Maturational Processes and the Facilitating Environment.* Madison, CT: International Universities Press, 1965, pp. 140–152.

—— (1971). *Playing and Reality.* London: Tavistock.

Wittgenstein, L. (1921). *Tractatus Logico-Philosophicus*, trans. D. Pears & D. McGuinness. Atlantic Highlands, NJ: Humanities Press, 1961.

—— (1953). *Philosophical Investigations*, 3rd ed., trans. G. Anscombe. New York: Macmillan.

Wolf, E. (1976). Ambiance and abstinence. *Annual of Psychoanalysis,* 4:101–115. Madison, CT: International Universities Press.

—— (1983). Aspects of neutrality. *Psychoanalytic Inquiry,* 3:675–690.

Wuellner, B. (1956). *Dictionary of Scholastic Philosophy.* Milwaukee: Bruce.

Index

101

About the Authors

Donna M. Orange, Ph.D., Psy.D. is a Supervising Analyst at the Institute for the Psychoanalytic Study of Subjectivity, New York, and the author of *Emotional Understanding* and *Peirce's Conception of God.*

George E. Atwood, Ph.D. is a founding faculty member of the Institute for the Psychoanalytic Study of Subjectivity, and Professor of Psychology at Rutgers University. He is coauthor of *Faces in a Cloud, Structures of Subjectivity* (TAP, 1984), *Psychoanalytic Treatment* (TAP, 1987), and *Contexts of Being* (TAP, 1992).

Robert D. Stolorow, Ph.D. is a Training and Supervising Analyst at the Institute of Contemporary Psychoanalysis, Los Angeles; a faculty member of the Institute for the Psychoanalytic Study of Subjectivity and Clinical Professor of Psychiatry, UCLA School of Medicine. His coauthored publications include *Faces in a Cloud, Psychoanalysis of Developmental Arrests, Structures of Subjectivity* (TAP, 1984), *Psychoanalytic Treatment* (TAP, 1987), and *Contexts of Being* (TAP, 1992). In 1995 he received the Distinguished Scientific Award from the Division of Psychoanalysis of the American Psychological Association.